Solution-Oriented Brief Therapy for Adjustment Disorders

A Guide for Providers Under Managed Care

Mental Health Practice Under Managed Care
A Brunner/Mazel Book Series

S. Richard Sauber, Ph.D., Series Editor

The Brunner/Mazel Mental Health Practice Under Managed Care Series addresses the major developments and changes resulting from the introduction of managed care. Volumes in the series will enable mental health professionals to provide effective therapy to their patients while conducting and maintaining a successful practice.

3. Solution-Oriented Brief Therapy for Adjustment Disorders: A Guide for Providers Under Managed Care
   By Daniel L. Araoz, Ed.D., and Marie A. Carrese, Ph.D.

2. Group Psychotherapy and Managed Mental Health Care: A Clinical Guide for Providers
   By Henry I. Spitz, M.D.

1. Psychopharmacology and Psychotherapy: Strategies for Maximizing Treatment Outcomes
   By Len Sperry, M.D., Ph.D.

Mental Health Practice Under Managed Care, Volume 3

Solution-Oriented Brief Therapy for Adjustment Disorders

A Guide for Providers Under Managed Care

Daniel L. Araoz, Ed.D.
and
Marie A. Carrese, Ph.D.

Brunner/Mazel *Publishers* • New York

Library of Congress Cataloging-in-Publication Data

Araoz, Daniel L.
Solution-oriented brief therapy for adjustment disorders: a guide for providers under managed care / Daniel L. Araoz and Marie A. Carrese.
p. cm. – (Mental health practice under managed care; v. 3)
Includes bibliographical references and index.
ISBN 0-87630-790-X (pbk.)
1. Adjustment disorders–Treatment. 2. Brief psychotherapy. 3. Solution-focused therapy. 4. Managed mental health care. I. Carrese, Marie A. II. Title. III. Series.
[DNLM: 1. Adjustment Disorders–therapy. 2. Psychotherapy, Brief–methods. 3. Adjustment Disorders–diagnosis. 4. Managed Care Programs–United States. WM 171 A662s 1996]
RC455.4.S87A73 1996
616.89' 14–dc20
DNLM/DLC
for Library of Congress 95-39445
CIP

Published by
BRUNNER/MAZEL, INC.
19 Union Square West
New York, New York 10003

Manufactured in the United States of America

10 9 8 7 6 5 4 3 2 1

To Karen, Lee, and my grandchild, Kaylee, who is the future.
DLA

To my siblings, Lena, Alex, Rose, Jeannie, and Fran.
MAC

Contents

FOREWORD BY JOSÉ J. LOPEZ, C.S.W. ix

1. *Practicing in the New Era of Managed Care* 1
2. *The Case of Mr. D.* 11
3. *Patient Impairment* 24
4. *Diagnosis* 34
5. *Adjustment and Personality* 49
6. *General Treatment Principles* 65
7. *Psychotherapy for Adjustment Disorders* 77
8. *Teaching Patients Self-Therapy* 104
9. *When Eight Sessions Are Not Enough* 124
10. *Spirituality as a Factor in the Writing of Reports for Managed Care Corporations* 135
11. *Conclusion* 148

REFERENCES 155

NAME INDEX 159

SUBJECT INDEX 160

Foreword

There is an Indian Proverb that says, "A journey of one thousand miles, begins with the first step." In this well written, highly organized, and focused "journey" through the diagnosis and treatment of adjustment disorders, the authors offer the clinician a "navigational map" through which to chart the course of the clinical intervention. This volume provides the clinician with a systematic format that will help to assess and treat this disorder. Incorporating the models of Lazarus' (1981) Multimodal Therapy and that of Goodman, Brown, & Deitz (1992), the authors provide the clinician with valuable tools in clearly identifying the nature of the adjustment disorder and the use of Solution-Oriented Brief Therapy as the appropriate model of treatment. The first step for clinicians is to embrace this model as an effective therapeutic intervention that will serve the best interest of the client.

There is wide agreement among most therapists that "good therapy" is one in which the client engages in a partnership with the therapist. The change process is client-driven and based on their actively participating in healing themselves. Through a holistic, and systemic perspective, the authors guide the clinician in formulating differential diagnostic assessments and arriving at a clear Adjustment Disorder classification. Tools that help to empower clients immediately, such as positive reframing, future questioning, and cognitive behavioral self management techniques are offered as first steps in engaging the client to assume responsibility for their therapy and change.

The authors are compassionate in viewing the client and the manifest symptom as "co-partners," where the symptom emerges as a functional impairment arising out of a maladaptive reaction to an identifiable psychosocial stressor. The time frame used in determining this diagnostic classification is based on the stressor having occurred no more than three months previously, with the duration of the symptoms/impairment not lasting for over six months.

The need to understand the diversity of cultural beliefs and the dimensional aspects of the human experience is critical to the belief that individuals have the capacity for self cure. It is important for the clinician to recognize the degree to which the manifest symptom of the client has already existed and that what creates the "client" is the inability to adjust to the new reality created by the psychosocial stressor. The authors are clear in advising the diagnostician to "maintain an open mind to understand and accept the reaction of patients to what has happened in their life." The clinician may not necessarily agree with the reaction, but can certainly offer clients other avenues, alternatives, or world views that will help them broaden and expand their intrapsychic "stage" for their drama to be played out. The clinician needs to be able to differentiate between "personality style" and a possible personality disorder and to respect the continuum of a style (tolerable to others) to an extreme behavior (intolerable to others). The clinician needs to view the life of clients' symptomatology through the lenses of their cultural values and belief systems in order to accurately determine a specific personality trait or disorder. The authors introduce the concept of "vivencia," which engages the client to reconstruct a "new experience," a new way to perceive the painful situation and to react to it.

At a time in the field of psychotherapy where professional accountability has become critical to our existence, this well organized manual is helpful in building our "professional armamentarium" to effectively negotiate the world of managed care. Although there has been resistance in the professional community to the perceived "arbitrary dispensing of sessions" and "threat to patient care," the hard fact is that managed care is now part of our "professional reality." As the authors point out from a business point of view: "These companies view the whole process of psychotherapy as a business transaction: The provider is the vendor, the product is the therapy, the client is the consumer, what the consumer pays is the profit, the ultimate aim of the whole operation is financial." Those clinicians who equip themselves with the tools required to provide brief therapy methods to their clients will inevitably be those clinicians utilized by managed care companies.

The authors have prepared a highly professional, well-organized "blueprint" for clinicians to be able to use in the assessment and treatment of adjustment disorders, while offering specific ways in which to handle the demands made by managed care programs. The authors clearly state their position that should the client require additional sessions beyond the eight sessions prescribed for short-term work, the clinician can objectively identify the need for further sessions. It is imperative, however, for the clinician to maintain clarity in the treatment objectives and goals to be achieved by the client. It is the professional responsibility of the clinician to advise and educate the managed care treatment reviewers so that they will understand the clients' vulnerability to regress without full mastery of the treatment plan.

The authors offer the clinician ample opportunity to broaden and expand the diagnostic criterion beyond adjustment disorder. Maintaining a watchful eye on other possible diagnostic avenues, the authors recommend that the clinician "keep the door open" when formulating a treatment plan. Clinicians need to assess the scope of diagnostic categories which proceed the classification of an adjustment disorder. Finally, the authors recommend group therapy as a model for post-treatment of adjustment disorders. The group provides ongoing support, correction through feedback, constructive criticism, a point of reference, and a forum for consultation.

Solution-Oriented Brief Therapy for Adjustment Disorders will surely be a "must have" reference book for the practitioner/clinician in treating AD and in effectively negotiating the world of managed care. It is a helpful tool that facilitates the first step of a long journey.

José J. Lopez, C.S.W.
Diplomate Clinical Social Work

Solution-Oriented Brief Therapy for Adjustment Disorders

A Guide for Providers Under Managed Care

1

Practicing in the New Era of Managed Care

In the Spring of 1994, the *Diagnostic and Statistical Manual of Mental Disorders, Fourth Edition*, of the American Psychiatric Association (DSM-IV) was finally published. Its predecessors, DSM-III (1980) and DSM-III-R (1987), established a systematic method to diagnose practically every possible condition treated by mental health practitioners, be they psychiatrists and psychiatric nurses, psychologists, social workers, mental health counselors, family therapists, or rehabilitation counselors.

The current DSM has refined and tightened up the diagnostic categories. For instance, in Cluster C of Personality Disorders (Axis II), the Passive Aggressive Personality Disorder, which was listed in the previous publications, does not appear. This deletion came in an effort to simplify diagnostic categories by establishing greater coordination with the *International Classification of Diseases* developed by the World Health Organization and because there was no sufficient empirical evidence "to warrant inclusion...as (an official category)...in DSM-IV" (p.703).

If a patient presents characteristic behaviors of Passive Aggressive Personality Disorder, it is included now under Personality Disorder "NOS" with the code 301.9.

In our specialization area of Adjustment Disorders, DSM-IV offers important changes as compared with its predecessor, DSM-III-R, which listed nine categories, including Adjustment Disorder *with physical complaints*, *with withdrawal*, and *with work (or academic) inhibition.* These three diagnostic categories have been deleted in DSM-IV, leaving the other six types of Adjustment Disorders. However, DSM-IV added the new specification of "Acute" and "Chronic" for qualifying each of the six listed categories.

THE CONSTRAINTS OF MANAGED CARE

This book follows DSM-IV in order to help the mental health practitioner in the new era of managed care. The current operative principle at work is a simple one: The provider is accountable for everything he/she does in the diagnosis and treatment of patients. Everything done clinically must be justified with precision and specificity. Therefore, gone are the amorphous "clinical judgment," the vague "long-term treatment," the general goal of working on "personality issues," and the evasive assessment of "the patient feeling better." Moreover, the clinician must be able to demonstrate *in advance* that a patient shows specific functional impairments that a specific treatment has been proven to be effective in curing. In other words, a treatment must be *specific* for resolving a *specific* type of impairment within a *specific* time frame.

Because of this emphasis on precision and specificity, careful attention is given to *functional impairment*: In what ways is the person requesting treatment unable to function to her/his satisfaction according to culturally reasonable expectations?

Thus, the symptoms must be measured along a continuum of functional impairment. Said differently, a practitioner cannot rely on his/her personal, professional judgment alone. The practitioner must abide by established criteria and guidelines set forth by the payers of mental health services, that is, the managed care and insurance companies. These criteria have become so stringent that to rebel against them will lead to the denial of reimbursement to the provider by the payers. For instance, a patient may not feel like going back to work after an accident but has no impairment recognized by the payer. In the past, therapy may have continued to help the patient "feel better." Now, further therapy would not be allowed.

These managed care companies view the whole process of psychotherapy as a business transaction: The provider is the vendor, the product is therapy, the client is the consumer, what the consumer pays is the profit, the ultimate aim of the whole operation is financial. The motivating question is: How can we increase the profit by providing quality service at the least expensive price?

By being part of this new system–and every mental health practitioner probably will be obligated to be part of it–the provider is forced to develop new, effective, brief therapy methods to help people get over their impairments quickly. The American way prevails even in mental health care–the quicker the better. Fast is better than slow.

But in spite of the nonclinical motivation of those who invented this system in which mental health practitioners are caught, there is something valuable in it. Everything that the mental health practitioner does must have a definite purpose and rationale. No more unfocused chatting during the first couple of sessions in order to establish rapport, for instance. Now, a precise identification of the impairment is the essential first step in order for the therapist to formulate the diagnosis of Adjustment Disorder (or of any other disorder, for that matter). This precise diagnosis will determine the specific, brief, and proven-effective treatment for one of the six types of Adjustment Disorder listed in DSM-IV.

Consequently, what we are facing is a redefinition of mental health care. No longer a private contract between patient and provider, mental health care is seen as *systemic*: Several providers organized in a system by a managed care company, work as a team, hopefully for the benefit of the patient, recognizing that physical and psychological problems are frequently linked and dependent on each other. The patient is treated in a system that, through its interaction, becomes–ideally–more effective than the isolated manner in which therapy was conducted in the past.

Think of patients with substance abuse habits or chronically depressed or with different types of phobias. In all these cases, a vicious cycle of symptom interdependency and influence is found. The symptoms feed themselves, producing new symptoms, both psychological and medical, within the personal system of the patient and affecting the functioning of the whole system: family, friends, work, and any other aspect of the patient's life.

This points to a crucial aspect of the mental health care system, as mentioned by Wylie (1994, p. 30): "The medical model itself is no longer the automatic reference point" of mental health care. In the medical model, the physician is in active control and, as the expert, tells the patient what she/he needs and prescribes medication and procedures of which the patient, most often, knows nothing. The physician even operates on the patient with little or no participation on the patient's part. The designation of *patient* is very appropriate: the recipient of the physician's ministrations, without active participation.

Psychotherapy, on the other hand, requires for its success the full understanding, cooperation, and commitment of the client, who is seen as the ultimate expert on his/her problem. Because of this, starting with Carl Rogers, the designation of *client* has been preferred by many nonmedical mental health providers. Client connotes active participation; patient indicates passivity.

MEDICALIZATION AND ADJUSTMENT DISORDERS

Client or patient, as conceptualizations, are not unimportant differences in mental health care. To become respected by physicians, many nonmedical mental health practitioners adopted the Aesculapian terminology. However, "medicalization" of psychotherapy can be considered the greatest error committed by the nonmedical mental health care providers because it weakens the need of the patient to be fully responsible for her/his recovery and to be committed to personal change through what he/she does in between therapy sessions. Therapy and psychotherapy are, themselves, misleading designations. Perhaps the ancient Buddhist term of *enlightenment* is more accurate. And enlightenment required the total commitment of the *disciple* (the one who learns), who was not a patient or client.

Especially when one deals with Adjustment Disorders, medicalization is counterproductive. By definition, Adjustment Disorders are functional impairments arising from the maladaptive reaction to an identifiable psychosocial stressor occurring at most three months previously. Even when the stressor and its consequences are terminated, the symptoms/impairment may continue, but not for over six months in order to be classified under Adjustment Disorder. It should be remembered that bereavement is not included among the stressors considered in order to diagnose Adjustment Disorder. Neither is this diagnosis given when anxiety or mood disorders are present; these correspond to a different type of Axis I disturbance listed in DSM-IV.

The above description of Adjustment Disorder, as we shall see in Chapter 4 on Diagnosis, includes the five criteria listed in DSM-IV. It is easy to understand that the overreaction producing the Adjustment Disorder is a function of beliefs and perception, fears, and expectations. This is basically a psychological phenomenon. Because of the very nature of Adjustment Disorders, to medicalize this condition is to aggravate it, complicate it, and prolong it.

To put this in practical terms, the functionally impaired overreaction to a psychosocial stressor manifests itself through many symptoms, physical and medical, as recognized in DSM-IV. The stressors that trigger the patient impairment are as numerous as the patients who seek help: termination of a job, retirement or a new occupation, a child leaving home during late adolescence, a serious accident or sickness, discovery of a marital infidelity, a sudden change in financial status, relocation to a different place, and so on and on.

CULTURAL VARIABLES

What creates the patient is the inability to adjust to the new reality established by the psychosocial stressor. The patient's maladaptive reaction becomes an overreaction, as measured by cultural norms and expectations. In other words, the reaction of the patient to the psychosocial stressor is not within the parameters of his/her culture. The patient's own culture considers his/her reaction to the psychosocial stressor inappropriate, extreme, strange, exaggerated, out of place, or simply wrong. "We don't do that," said by people of the same culture as the patient, is the typical reaction indicating cultural disapproval.

The cultural dimension of adjustment to a new reality, usually painful and difficult to accept for those of a different culture, presents areas that must be handled delicately and respectfully with tolerance and acceptance, if not with agreement. This is especially true in the U.S.A., where so many world cultures mix and intermingle. DSM-IV (1994), in the section on Adjustment Disorders (p. 625), makes a special effort to remind the diagnostician of the cultural dimension. Because of this, it is worthwhile to pay close attention to the actual text. It recommends that the cultural context of the individual be considered in order to decide whether the patient's reaction to the psychosocial stressor is within the expectations and parameters of that culture. The clinician must determine if the response is viewed as inappropriate in the patient's culture or, on the contrary, if it is appropriate and expected, even though other cultures (the clinician's?) may consider it maladaptive and objectionable. The clinician needs humility to recognize one's cultural limitations. The patient's reaction, by the way, includes the intensity of upset experienced and the length of time it takes the patient to revert to "normal" functioning. The text emphasizes the real cultural differences of stressors and reactions to them.

This means that psychosocial stressors, in and of themselves, are neither positive nor negative. "All depends on the color of the lens through which it is viewed," the lens being the cultural context, in the words of the classic Spanish poet, Ramon the Campoamor. Cultural sensitivity means that the diagnostician has a mind open to understanding and accepting the reaction of the patient to what has happened in his/her life (not necessarily to agree with that reaction). In this respect, if a person is brought to an emergency room by her neighbors because after the death of her husband she tried to commit suicide, it is imperative to find out whether this reaction is accepted within the patient's cultural system. If so, rather than to consider the woman pathological and treat her as such, the mental health practitioner has to find alternatives to suicide accepted by the woman's culture.

All of us are so deeply conditioned by our culture that it is necessary to train ourselves in order to be able to perceive things differently. What is bad in one culture may be good in another. The younger daughter who is not allowed to marry because she must care for her aging mother accepts her role with pride in some Latin cultures. In middle America, this young woman would be considered unassertive, having low self-esteem, and overly dependent on her mother and family.

The young wife who sacrifices herself after the death of her husband is honored and admired in some Hindu cultures, while we would tend to identify serious pathology in her behavior.

The older son accepting a celibate life in order to enter the Catholic priesthood stands above the rest of the children in the family and is nearly worshipped in some cultures. Our culture may tend to view this type of celibacy with suspicions about the young man's mental health.

In the middle-class American culture, the failure to purchase life insurance is for many people a sign of irresponsibility. But in other cultures, buying life insurance is an insult to the parents' families and demonstrates a serious lack of trust in them. If the parents die, the relatives take care of the children as if they were their own. If one spouse dies, the family helps the remaining parent to take care of his/her family. Because of this, godparents are exceedingly important and highly respected.

Finally, in some cultures, suicide became an honorable ritual intended to resolve problems that impinge on personal or family honor. The person who ended his/her life in the prescribed manner was worthy of praise, glory, and dignity and his/her relatives' name was enhanced by this act. Our culture, on the other hand, finds it very hard to justify any type of suicide.

In the first three examples, the psychosocial stressor for a middle-of-the-road American person would be intolerable, while it is not viewed as a stressor at all within each culture. The culture's attitude about life and living changes the perception of the same event or circumstances. As a matter of fact, there is such tremendous social pressure in those cultures that *not* to do what is expected could put the three young people of the previous illustrations under almost unbearable stress.

These are instances of what DSM-IV calls "the context of the individual's cultural setting" (p. 625). Not to act as indicated would be maladaptive in those cultures. We can imagine a host of symptoms–real functional impairment–in those young people had they refused to follow traditional custom. We can also imagine the surprise of these young people, not making any sense of our "objections" to what for them is culturally correct and "normal."

What follows from all the above is that there is no *natural* nor logical relation between the stressor and the reaction to it. The 45-year-old man who loses his eyesight in an accident can become so upset about it that he ends up clinically depressed and suicidal. He can also adjust to the new, difficult, and painful reality of his life and become an expert in Braille. The woman who underwent a massive mastectomy and later finds out that a less invasive surgical procedure would have been appropriate may end up bitter, cynical and sarcastic with everybody. She may also become a crusader for ecological health and health care issues.

In these two examples, the *disorder* of adjustment is the negative and unproductive reaction to the stressor, while the constructive and positive reaction is culturally accepted and socially beneficial. Consequently, the latter enhances the individual and provides an opportunity for personal and psychological growth while establishing her/him more strongly within the community.

By definition, also, Adjustment Disorder is a passing condition. When it continues for over six months, another diagnosis is warranted, be it on Axis I, such as Mood Disorders, Somatoform Disorders, Anxiety Disorders, or even a Psychotic Disorder, or on Axis II, such as Personality Disorders, especially of Cluster A. The fact that Adjustment Disorders are passing disturbances presents a special challenge for Counseling Psychologists like the authors because Counseling Psychology specializes in normal, everyday obstacles to personal growth and effective functioning. Managed care corporations know this and expect *brief therapy* for its cure.

Research has shown that brief therapy is, indeed, the treatment of choice for Adjustment Disorder, as will be discussed in Chapter 5. It is obvious that an accurate diagnosis is essential, as Chapter 4 will elaborate. But once there is a correct diagnosis of Adjustment Disorder, there is no indication for the use of medication. Indeed, in most cases, medication is counterproductive, lessening patients' motivation to be responsible for their maladaptive reaction to the psychosocial stressor that elicited the impairment. Medication weakens their resolve to correct with effective action the overreaction which produces the functional impairment. These patients do not require medication. They do need the therapist's direct guidance, support, and reinforcement in order to alter and correct their maladaptive reaction. They need the therapist in order to discover more satisfying ways to adjust to situations beyond their control, like the ones mentioned earlier.

Therefore, therapy for Adjustment Reaction, the subject matter of Chapter 5, must be a highly skilled intervention, focused on concrete goals, involving the patient in active "homework" and "self-therapy" in between sessions and utilizing means to measure progress behaviorally at the four levels to be discussed in Chapter 3: biopsychology, intimate relations, people interaction, and future orientation.

WHAT THIS BOOK OFFERS

This volume provides a working manual for effective interventions in the treatment of Adjustment Disorders. It provides general principles rather than strict prescriptions, taking the mental health practitioner step by step, from initial contact and diagnosis to treatment, assessment of progress, and termination. It provides effective but broad guidelines in order to enhance the quality of the psychotherapeutic intervention. It makes it easier for the clinician to operate systematically and systemically for the benefit of the patient with a diagnosis of Adjustment Disorder.

Our suggestion to the reader who wishes to benefit maximally from this manual is, first, to page through it in order to become familiar with its contents.

Second, to read the case of Mr. D. in Chapter 2 since in it are found all the essentials of treating Adjustment Disorders effectively and briefly.

Third, to become very comfortable with Chapter 3 in order to learn the way of perceiving the patient's problem from the managed care companies' point of view.

Fourth, to understand thoroughly Chapters 4 and 5 with the intention of feeling perfectly at ease with the diagnosis of Adjustment Disorder.

Fifth, to study–not just to read–Chapters 6 and 7 in order to be able to quickly use a multitude of techniques related to Adjustment Disorders.

Sixth, to be familiar with Chapter 9 in case patients need more than the "prescribed" limited number of therapy sessions.

Finally, after having acquired this familiarity with the book, to consult it when any question arises about diagnosis, treatment, or report writing.

It is our hope that *Solution-Oriented Brief Therapy for Adjustment Disorders* will help you to use your talents as a psychotherapist more fully when you treat patients diagnosed as having this problem. In these cases, you can be most effective as a *mental health* provider, not as a *medical* practitioner, as discussed earlier.

These patients need you to help them discover new and creative ways to cope with their frightening life situation. They are confused and in emotional pain arising from unexpected changes in their personal "world." Their familiar reality has been disrupted and they do not know how to proceed. Your therapeutic interventions will give them a new lease on life and open up new vistas to enjoy life again–indeed, to enjoy life even more in spite of the changes, the psychosocial stressors, that have upset their life style and have complicated the comfortable and familiar ways of previous functioning.

In a true sense, you will become their teacher–"A teacher for a day can become a parent for a lifetime," is what an ancient Taoist saying states–and their midwife to a new life since one of the many mysteries of living is that many unhappy experiences may turn out to be blessings in disguise in the long run.

Your job is noble, enhancing and empowering. This book is here to help you accomplish it more effectively. Let us accompany you in this unique and wonderful task.

2

The Case of Mr. D.

When the secretary answered the telephone, a rough voice, unfriendly and short, requested an appointment. She asked a few general questions required–correct spelling of the name, phone number, referral source, availability for an appointment, and summary nature of the problem. Mr. D. sounded very angry when he responded that he had no *problem.* "I know how to solve my own problems and need no damn doctor to solve them for me," he said, and added, "I want to see the doctor. Period. The nature of the problem (mimicking the secretary) is none of your damn business." When she answered, "I'm sorry. Of course you'll want to tell the doctor yourself," he replied. "My, my, my! I see you are well trained. You don't let yourself respond to my style. Congratulations!"

That was Mr. D.'s first contact with the office. After being difficult about the first appointment, he agreed to a day and time. He gave the referral source as a psychologist in a neighboring town who, as it turned out, had been the therapist for Mr. D.'s wife in the past.

The day of the appointment, Mr. D. arrived 50 minutes early, "In case the doctor can see me ahead of time," as he put it. The secretary explained that the doctor would be busy until the scheduled time for Mr. D. While he was waiting, he showed great restlessness, pacing back and forth, sitting down and taking a magazine to read, but flipping through its pages rapidly instead; then taking another one, throwing it back on the end table and returning to his pacing. He went to the bathroom three times during his long wait. Because the clinician shares the office suite with other psychotherapists, four other patients arrived during the time Mr. D. was waiting, sat for a few minutes, and then went into the offices areas, behind a general door. Each time a patient went in, Mr. D. came to the secretary's desk to inquire if Dr. Y. would see him now and each time she reminded him that his appointment was for later.

Finally, he was ushered into Dr. Y.'s office. His first remark was that Dr. Y. was younger than he expected. Inviting him to sit down, Dr. Y., smiling, asked him if that was really important to him. Mr. D., without sitting down yet, responded with manifest arrogance that experience is the most important asset in life and that he had plenty of it, ending by looking at Dr. Y. condescendingly and calling him, "Sonny." Dr. Y. ignored the insult and repeated the invitation to Mr. D. to sit down, to which he replied, "I'll sit down when I'm good and ready."

At this point, Dr. Y. stated calmly and with a friendly smile, "You called to see me. I'm sure you want to get right to the point. Please, tell me now what brought you here." His reply was not conciliatory. "If you know that I don't want to waste time, you must be reading my mind. So, go on, tell me more about myself. Go on." Dr. Y. simply responded, "I give up, Mr. D. You seem to want to start a fight and I refuse to cooperate. What brought you here?"

This finally worked. Mr. D. smiled for the first time, saying that he was testing Dr. Y. and that he was satisfied with the outcome. He added that he was truly concerned about the age difference between doctor and patient, to which Dr. Y. asked him how much he knew about him. The patient confessed he knew only that he was a psychologist and that, yes, he was curious about his experience. When Mr. D. found out that Dr. Y. had worked as a management consultant for business corporations, Mr. D. showed some interest, even though he made several disparaging remarks about consultants who have never run a company. Dr. Y. refused to argue and reminded him that he was not going to get into a fight. Mr. D. backed down and after a few more questions about Dr. Y.'s experience, he started to talk about himself, though still defensively and in a nonfriendly manner.

He emphasized that he did not believe in doctors and that he was here under duress, that he was giving Dr. Y. one chance (no more than three visits) to prove to him that this "psychotherapy" (spitting out the word) was worth his while. Dr.Y. agreed with the patient that even in one session he should experience some improvement. With what he was going to learn in these visits, Mr. D. would be able to reengineer himself, according to his own blueprints, his own goals. But he had to practice what he learned. Today he was going to learn what he could practice tomorrow. Yes, indeed, Dr. Y. did not want to waste time. He did not ask him about his "problem" but simply inquired, "What comes to mind when you think of what brought you here?" After trying to fight and stating that nothing came to mind, Mr. D. became reflective and admitted that he had never paid attention to this.

In a calmer and friendlier tone of voice, he explained that for many years he had wanted to retire early. But things kept happening at work that delayed his decision. The more he had to wait, the more excited he became about finally doing it. Last year he was almost ready to sell his electrical parts manufacturing company. The deal failed at the last minute and he had to start all over again, finding a new buyer, going through all the aggravation of lawyers and endless meetings and negotiation. Finally, it happened. He was still only 64. One year earlier than regular retirement. Still, he had accomplished his goal of early retirement. "I almost didn't do it. But I feel great that it happened before 65, even though my dream was to retire at 60." The deal had been very profitable and he sold his company "for more money than I would have paid," as he stated with obvious pride.

When asked what he had dreamed of doing after retirement, he became enthusiastic. He had thought a lot about these things, five of them in all. He was a jazz aficionado and he had a good ear for music, but never had he had the time to learn how to play a musical instrument. He dreamt of playing the clarinet and he wanted to do it. He would give himself two years to learn it well enough to play in public. He also had a list of almost 20 books that he wanted to read, some current but most of them classic books that he had never been able to read in college or later. The third goal for his retirement was an extended trip to Europe. He had been there many times, alone and with his wife, mostly on business. However, he had not been able to visit some of "the gem cities," as he called them, Vienna, Prague, Budapest, and Krakow. He had looked forward to his retirement to go there just for pleasure, without having to call his business every day as he used to do when he owned his company.

Mr. D. had two other dreams that he had thought out in careful detail. One was to teach sailing to deprived youngsters in Florida. He owned his own 45-foot boat docked in Port St. Lucie. His dream was to advertise his sailing program through his church or through the area schools so that he could get three or four youngsters who showed some kind of promise and teach them how to become expert sailors. The second dream, similar to this, was to advertise in his church that he was available to the members of his congregation for consultation on private business matters. He wanted to try these two "services" to others, without expecting any monetary reward. He said, "I was lucky in life. I feel an obligation to help others now with what I have acquired." He had dreamt of doing these two things on a continuing basis, devoting one day a week to each during the months that he lived in Florida.

Then he explained what had happened. "As you can see, my plans were well thought out. I knew what I was going to do in my golden years (he used this expression often). But then came this strange reaction, completely unexpected." He gave important details. His retirement party was a big event with over 500 people in attendance, the best hotel, the best food, the best band. People gave speeches that made Mr. D. feel wonderful and presented him with expensive gifts. Two days after the party, he and his wife started a 14-day sailing vacation in the Caribbean. He had felt great during these days, as he was an enthusiastic sailor and everything had gone "like clockwork."

Then he settled down to start his new life in the house that he loved, having built it to his specifications 10 years earlier in the best area of Port St. Lucie. But two weeks after returning from the sailing trip, all the restlessness, anxiety, fears, and lack of concentration started. He remembered that Saturday when he got up early and felt "strange." Initially, he tried to ignore his discomfort and forced himself to act as if nothing were different. But it got harder every day. By the beginning of the third week, he was getting really worried. This is when he admitted that something was wrong and called his old high school friend Jim, a physician who had moved to Florida about 12 years earlier and continued to practice general medicine just a couple of days a week. They had been close friends for over 40 years and enjoyed many things in common, as did both families. Mr. D.'s two children, a 35-year-old businessman, the father of two little girls, and a 33-year-old daughter, an attorney very devoted to her work and single, both living in New York City, had grown up with Jim's three children and were still very good friends, as were Jim's wife and his wife.

Over the telephone, Jim prescribed a daily dose of 10 mg of Valium and 20 mg. of BuSpar, both reliable antianxiety medications, though not often prescribed conjointly. His wife, meanwhile, worried about her husband taking drugs, recommended that he go into psychotherapy. He was against the idea and Jim assured him that the medication would do the trick and that he did not need psychotherapy. His wife had used therapy on and off for the last 12 years and insisted that he should consult with a therapist about his retirement. Mr. D. kept repeating that there was nothing to consult about and that his symptoms were like a passing headache. After he had taken the medications as prescribed for just over four weeks, there was no significant relief of his anxiety, worries, and inability to concentrate. As a matter of fact, he had to admit that he was feeling worse. Therefore, he gave in to his wife and reluctantly, after a few days of delay, he called Dr. Y. and made the appointment.

By the time of the first session, he had been "different," as he called it, for almost two months. The initial anger and animosity during the first encounter with the therapist reflected his frustration and humiliation at needing help to resolve his own problems. His demand to be done with therapy in three sessions came more from the need to protect his self-image as a self-sufficient man than out of antagonism to therapy. Dr. Y.'s expert handling of Mr. D. won him over to therapy as a learning *process* rather than a medical or psychological treatment. When the patient asked about his diagnosis by inquiring, "So, what do you think is going on with me at this time," Dr. Y. explained Adjustment Disorder in terms of previous learning, expectations, and circumstances that affect one's perception, attitude, or thinking mode, and, consequently, feelings and behavior.

Before ending the first session, Dr. Y. gave Mr. D. very concrete prescriptions, as the Initial Report in Chapter 10 shall indicate. He was given a self-improvement book to read entitled *Reengineering Yourself* (Araoz & Sutton, 1994), asked to come up with concrete plans to start achieving his retirement goals, and encouraged to concentrate on these plans and goals when he started to worry. All this was summarized in three words: *Read*, *Plan*, *Switch*. He was also told that the therapist would go over these three items with him during the next visit.

The therapy notes taken during the second visit, a week later, and transcribed at the end of Chapter 10 speak for themselves. Of the three prescriptions given, the patient had (1. *Read*) started to read the book, (2. *Plan*) taken concrete steps in two areas of his original retirement plans, and (3. *Switch*) practiced some of the mind exercises from the book. By accomplishing all these things, he, first of all, confirms the diagnosis of Adjustment Disorder; second, he gives the clinician evidence to assess the prognosis; and third, he confirms the validity of the treatment plan and approach for this particular patient.

The advantage of working in line with the principles of Solution-Oriented Brief Therapy (SOBT) is that the patient is given the opportunity to start taking responsibility for the course of treatment from the very beginning. Unlike other ways of thinking theoretically, SOBT does not suspect initial progress as "flight into health," but considers it as evidence of the patient's capability to change. Obviously, the improvement will be monitored carefully in the following weeks. This was Dr. Y.'s rationale for setting the third appointment two weeks after the second.

However, one's eye should continuously be on the original diagnosis. To repeat once more a basic principle of psychological treatment, if the patient does not respond without having a solid reason for it, the diagnosis of Adjustment Disorder must be reviewed.

By the third session, which Mr. D. wanted to have one week after the second and Dr. Y. insisted on having two weeks later in order to give him "time to practice what he was learning from the book" he was reading, the first setback had taken place. The patient reported that for about 10 days after the second session everything was moving ahead smoothly. Then, one cold, dreary morning, he got up feeling like before: restless, nervous, worried, "but I could not 'Switch.' I got stuck in this mood for the rest of the day." He went back to the book to review some of the mind exercises, without good results. He even had thought of calling Dr. Y. as the latter had suggested, during the first visit, that he should do if he had any questions, but he had decided against that course of action "because my appointment was coming in only four more days." However, he went through three very miserable days and showed up for the third session visibly altered. During the first two visits, he was neatly dressed, carefully groomed, and showing a high level of energy–talking firmly and loudly, moving briskly, thinking clearly. This time, all these traits were reversed. He started by saying, slowly and in a low tone of voice, "This is not working. I guess Jim (his physician friend) was right when he told me that I did not need psychotherapy." Then he explained what had happened.

Dr. Y. took an unworried attitude, not allowing himself to be drawn by the patient's negativism, and reverted to the learning model. Students have setbacks, things often don't move at the pace we expect, etc. He also emphasized that the progress Mr. D. had experienced in the first few weeks was true and real and that he refused to ignore it. In their effort to understand the circumstances of the setback, the fact came up that Mrs. D. had gone to visit her sister in Atlanta for a long weekend the day before he woke up with the recurrence of the original symptoms. Surprisingly enough, he had not made any connection between the two events. Now that Dr. Y. brought this up, the patient refused to accept any link between them, saying that his wife had traveled many times to Atlanta in the past and that he had never minded it, but rather thought that this change was a good break for the two of them, and so on, still refusing to associate his wife's trip of five days with the recurrence of his symptoms.

His wife had left the evening before he woke up feeling so upset. She was supposed to return the day of the third appointment. Dr. Y. asked him to imagine that he was feeling the way he had before the setback; he instructed him to close his eyes and make believe that he was back two weeks thinking about his retirement goals, planning the European trip, and so on, feeling wonderful physically, emotionally, and spiritually. The image suggested was that of energy filling him like a soothing light that penetrated every part of him, especially his brain, purifying, strengthening, healing, and becoming stronger with every breath of air he took. This technique was continued for several minutes until Mr. D. started to feel noticeably better.

Next he was reminded that all students experience setbacks when they are learning a new skill and he should now imagine himself–plan in his mind–going home, taking care of everything he had neglected during the last three days, especially himself, and getting the house ready for his wife's arrival that evening. Dr. Y. guided him through this mental rehearsal, adding the same suggestion of the energy light of the previous practice.

After these two exercises, patient and therapist talked about the details of getting himself *cheerfully ready* for his wife's return. Then Dr. Y. reverted to the retirement projects and asked Mr. D. what he would do in order to make up for the four days lost. They discussed this in a lighthearted way and by then the session was almost over. Dr. Y. ended it by asking Mr. D. concretely, "So, what'll you do until we see each other next time?" The patient recited what he intended to do: first, repeat at home today the mind exercises he had practiced during this session and get the house ready for his wife's return that evening; second, go back to reading the self-improvement book; third, continue his efforts to volunteer his services through his church; fourth, pick up where he had left off before the setback regarding the practice exercises proposed by the book. All these were to be recorded daily.

Before leaving, with his mood visibly improved, and remarking that he had to shave and "get dressed," Mr. D. asked what his condition was all about. Dr. Y. responded that his was a common reaction to retirement, technically called "adjustment disorder with anxiety," and that it had a very good prognosis. This *label* seemed to give him a type of temporary identity to hold on to. However, feeling better as he did, the patient wanted to end "the consultations" right then and there, saying that he would call Dr. Y. if he had another question. The clinician responded that a fourth, follow-up visit, face to face, in order to analyze how well he had recovered from the setback was advisable and the smart thing to do. He added that progress would be measured as a function of his outcome objectives and of his mastering of the new skills, especially those under "Switch" in the formula "Read, Plan, Switch" of the first session.

However, he was willing to compromise as long as Mr. D. promised to telephone him in two weeks to report on his progress. Consequently, no appointment was made for another session.

It should be noticed that even though Dr. Y. perceived a relationship between the patient's setback and his wife's five-day trip, he did not persist in convincing him of it. However important this was in order for an understanding of the powerful emotional support that his wife offered him, it does not become a treatment goal unless it directly affects the restoration of behavioral functioning that the impairment had suppressed.

The second observation is that Dr. Y.'s emphasis on learning and practicing new skills was used as a technique to avoid the patient's resistance to treatment. Even though Adjustment Disorder is a distinct condition, subtly differentiated from similar dysfunctions, there was no need for the therapist to be as specifically accurate with the patient as he had to be with the managed care company involved in this case.

Two weeks later, Mr. D. called to make another appointment with Dr. Y. He sounded positive, firm, and factual when he stated, in passing, that he was happy with his progress and that he was looking forward to seeing Dr. Y. Due to circumstances, the appointment was made for a week later. By the time of the fourth session, three whole weeks had elapsed since the third visit.

Mr. D. reported in detail the progress he had made. The three-month trip to Europe was all arranged for the following spring and paid for. After talking to a different minister than the first one he had visited, he had committed himself to the two voluntary activities that he had talked about. Not only had these been announced in the church bulletin, but three youngsters had already registered for the sailing lessons and one young businessman had made an appointment to consult with him about problems he had with marketing. He said that *Reengineerinq Yourself* had become his bible and he practiced the exercises in the book regularly. Finally, he had bought a clarinet and started weekly lessons with a retired jazz musician of some note who was a great teacher. All this he had done without wasting time, as he said, and in order to catch up after the setback of almost a month before.

Asked about any other setback, Mr. D. reported that only on

three occasions had he started to feel a little anxious, but that he had been able to short-circuit (his term) the negative mood without too much effort. Asked how he had done this, he referred to some of the exercises in the book regarding "power thoughts" and creativity. This gave the clinician a fairly good assurance that the impairment produced by the retirement was now corrected and that Mr. D. would be able to continue to function normally again, utilizing his energy to lead a full life, according to his values and goals.

After summarizing what had happened during the weeks that they had known each other, Mr. D. stated that he wanted to retain Dr. Y. as a personal consultant. He wanted to call or visit him about once a month, as he believed the book recommended, in order to discuss his progress. Dr. Y. accepted the proposal and Mr. D. took his leave.

In the following six months, Mr. D. saw Dr. Y. seven times, always as a "consultant," not a therapist, and to report on what he was doing or to discuss points from *Reengineerinq Yourself*, the book that had become "my owner's manual," in his words. After this, he continued to see Dr. Y. every two or three months. In the two years since his first contact, he has missed only three months without seeing Dr. Y., not counting the three months during which he took the vacation trip to Europe. Lately, he had admitted that this process with Dr. Y. was therapy but not the type he objected to, with weekly or biweekly visits and a dependency on the therapist as if the patient were helpless. He added that he had been "too frightened" when his symptoms began to admit his need for treatment, help, and a cure.

In cases like this in which the individual does not have a personality disorder, it is rather typical to note dramatic progress in patients with Adjustment Disorder diagnosis. Three conditions are required: first, that the case be *acute* rather than *chronic*, following the useful distinction based on DSM-IV, p. 625, when one is dealing with the course of AD; second, that there be no evidence of a personality *disorder*, regardless of the patient's personality style, as considered in Chapter Five; and last, that the treatment be Solution-Oriented Brief Therapy (SOBT), including cognitive, behavioral, and self-hypnotic methods and techniques, as Dr. Y. employed with Mr. D.

This case is instructive because Mr. D. gave the initial impression of being almost out of touch with reality, coming to the first appointment almost an hour early and bothering the receptionist several times with questions about the possibility of being seen ahead of the scheduled hour.

However, Dr. Y. confirmed the initial diagnosis of AD with anxiety (309.24) made at intake. The HMO plan to which Mr. D. belonged, like many others, gives an extensive telephone interview when the patient calls in for service. But unlike many managed care companies, this HMO employed as telephone intake workers highly skilled mental health professionals who established the initial diagnosis or made suggestions on the direction to move during the first session in order to come up with a workable diagnosis.

The stressor responsible for the patient's maladaptive reaction was his retirement and the change of life style produced by it, designated by DSM-IV (pp. 623 and 625) as *acute*, opposed to chronic, and as a *single event*, contrasted to *multiple stressors.*

Once the clinician was sure of the diagnosis, he was able to proceed firmly, establishing concrete goals and objectives. As we shall discuss in Chapter 9, following the language of the *Consolidated Standards Manual* (see Joint Commission, 1991), the *goals* in this case were the five activities that the patient came up with for his retirement years. The *objectives* were the specific means taken by the patient in order to attain those five goals within a reasonably short period of time.

Coupled with this SOBT approach was the serious monitoring of the patient's progress by means of his reporting on the prescriptions given each session. The accommodation to the patient who was leery of "therapy" and the reframing of therapy into a learning process for which consultation with a consultant was warranted were beneficial in engaging Mr. D. Resistance was not a functional concept for Dr. Y. What others would call resistance, he considered a call to present things differently to the patient.

If one were dealing with a case of AD due to a chronic stressor, such as living with a severely retarded child, the whole therapeutic approach would be different. An even stronger emphasis would be placed on the behavioral changes needed and a close monitoring of the patient's negative self-hypnosis would be required. For instance, one of several crucial and practical manifestations to consider on the behavioral end is whether the patient, deceiving himself/herself under the guise of love, is doing more for the retarded child than is needed because it is easier to do so, rather than doing things for the child that are absolutely necessary.

As for the self-hypnosis, one of the many important aspects to consider is to ask if the patient is fostering negative, self-pitying, and angry feelings, while ignoring other positive aspects of his/her life. When the individual states that s/he has had enough, the clinician can help the patient tap inner resources, such as to get in touch with the stronger self in order not to be dominated by the ineffective part of the self. Finally, the patient will do well in a therapy group formed by other parents of retarded children that may become a continuous source of support and a network of resources for many years to come.

It is trite to state that no two clinical cases are the same. But it is important to remember this truism when dealing with a new patient. And that is the main reason why in SOBT or any other brief therapy method careful planning is essential for the successful management of the case. The Initial Report for Mr. D. in Chapter 10 contains the treatment plan, not under a separate heading but implicitly in the *Prescriptions* section, which comes directly from the *Impairment*, *Severity*, and *Diagnosis* sections. Some managed care companies require a specific and precise treatment plan. In this case, as Chapter 9 points out, the advice of Goodman et al. (1992) is wise regarding the initial need for leaving the door open, as it were, for additional interventions and/or changes in clinical procedures through the use of a statement like, "May have to be modified pending further data."

With Mr. D., a possible treatment intervention could have been, for example, one or more sessions with his wife if, after the first session, new evidence had appeared showing an unhealthy overdependency on her. Since this was not the case, the initial treatment plan, consisting of the practical means to be taken by the patient in the next few weeks in order to achieve his retirement goals, remained unchanged. The point we want to stress is that Dr. Y.'s Initial Report in Chapter 10 did not close any doors for future modifications, additions, or subtractions in the proposed treatment procedures.

In this case, the clinician proceeded in a professionally planned and methodical manner in order to obtain solid therapeutic results quickly. And, to emphasize it once more, an accurate diagnosis is at the center of any effective treatment. Had Mr. D. not responded in the manner in which he did, the only possible decision would have been to modify the original diagnosis, recognizing that what appeared as Adjustment Disorder initially was indeed a different type of pathological condition, probably in the Mood Disorders family.

3

Patient Impairment

DSM-IV refers frequently to "impairment of function." The concept is operative in the age of managed care and fits most appropriately with the strict demands for accountability.

In this structure, the purpose of psychotherapy is to restore the patient at least to the previous level of functioning, when therapy was not required. Patients seek therapy because they are aware of symptoms or manifestations of impaired functioning. Therapy will do away with the symptoms and allow them to function in a satisfying way, enjoying life and feeling basically good about themselves. Goodman, Brown, and Deitz (1992) have developed and explained this concept thoroughly and comprehensively. They state emphatically:

> Impairments are the reasons why a patient requires treatment. They are not the reasons for the presence of the disorder, nor are they the disorder itself. Rather they are observable, objectifiable manifestations that necessitate and justify care. (p. 31)

They further use an apt metaphor to explain that "impairments are 'behavioral windows' into the aberrant biochemical phenomena and psychological variations of existence that are the etiology of psychiatric disorders" (p. 31).

In other words, they indicate that without functional impairment on the part of the individual there is no justification for therapy and that functional impairments or symptoms are manifestations of an existing "disorder." Their thinking goes along the postpsychoanalytical model endorsed by cognitive behaviorism, which, in an overly simplified way, may be stated as follows:

> The symptom is the problem, regardless of how or why the symptom developed. Controlling the symptom corrects the situation even though the origin of the symptom may never be known. In order to make symptoms disappear, the patient must be helped to change "thinking" and behavior.

Psychiatrist Edelstien (1990) reminds us that each of the numerous theories attempting to explain the origins of psychiatric symptoms or maladaptive behavior presents "precious little specific evidence" (p. 3), that will justify its explanations. Yet, in spite of this, many therapists adhere fervently to their theories as if they were absolutely proven and true. According to Edelstien, they use three maneuvers: First, they appeal to authority; second, they present the information that the patient reveals during therapy, supposedly confirming their theory; and, third, they stress "the proof" of the theory as provided by successful cases they have treated, though Edelstien wonders how accurate these positive reports really are.

The appeal to authority is based on what the originator of each theory has stated. It is assumed that because he/she has created the theory, it is a correct theory–circular thinking at its best! The confirmation of the theory from patients' reactions during treatment, Edelstien continues, is also faulty. If patients do not respond in accordance with the theory held by the therapist, so it goes, the patient displays "resistance." The self-talk of the therapist seems to be something like this: "If you don't do what I expect or if you disagree with me, you're resisting." Then, what is not "resistance" is collected as evidence in support of the theory. Finally, successful cases do not prove a theory, as Edelstien (1990) remarks: "Therapists with very different theories are also claiming successes, and all indications are that they are having them in equal proportions" (p. 6).

Because of these considerations, we regard theory as an operative instrument, a map to follow, in order to proceed in an orderly manner in psychotherapy. By no means do we view theory as a final explanation of anything that contributes to people changing. Consequently, we too go along with the practical approach of current managed care policy stating that functional impairments are the focus of therapy and the only justification for therapy. In this regard, we present a model based on Lazarus' (1981) Multimodal Therapy, later in this chapter.

The second model is that of Goodman et al. (1992). They propose a useful conceptualization of functional impairment at four levels of functioning, centered on ***biopsychology***, by which they mean the patient's internal world. Closest to this center is the next level of *intimacy* (in their words, "the sphere of family and significant other" p. 35). Next comes the larger area of ***people interaction***. They call it "interpersonal" interaction, but because intimacy is also interpersonal, we prefer "people" in a more general way. Lastly, impairments occur in the area of ***future orientation***, or, according to Goodman et al., "future/achievement." Each of these spheres has its own set of impairments and their book presents useful tables (pp. 34–37) with which responsible clinicians should be familiar. As far as we know, they are the first ever to introduce the P.I.P., or Patient Impairment Profile. The two models will be explained in the next section.

TWO PATIENT IMPAIRMENT MODELS

To talk about patient impairments without having a grid into which to place them becomes confusing. This is why we are offering two different but similar models. The first one is an adaptation of Lazarus' (1981) Multimodal Behavior Therapy which identifies seven areas of human functioning, using the acronym BASIC I.D. This stands for *B*ehavior, *A*ffect, *S*ensations, *I*mages, *C*ognition, *I*nterpersonal relations and *D*iet (including drugs). Lazarus uses "D" for Drugs but includes under it "nutrition, hygiene, exercise and the panoply of medical diagnoses and interventions that affect personality" (p. 13).

Patient impairments, therefore, can be arranged along these seven areas in an orderly fashion. Thus, in the case of Mr. D. in Chapter 2, the initial Patient Impairment Profile (P.I.P.) would look like this:

Behavior:	Lack of concentration, inability to stay put for more than a few minutes.
Affect:	Insecurity, worries, fears, feeling like a loser with nothing to live for.
Sensations:	Restless, nervous, tense, with muscular pains in legs and back.
Images:	Of lack of money, sickness, doom (most of the time).

Cognition:	Can't use rational mind for long.
Interpersonal:	Less social contacts since "event," very irritable with wife, neglects contact with adult children and friends.
Diet:	No medication now, erratic eating habits, wakes up at night "worrying," then can't go back to sleep for several hours, no regular exercise.

As can be seen, all the symptoms or functional impairment for which Mr. D. decided finally to request professional help appear in a systematic and orderly way, making it easy to proceed in therapy with definite goals in mind. The symptoms may be listed under more than one category, so that there is frequent overlap in the seven areas of the BASIC I.D., clarifying the picture of the patient's problems and the concrete goals for psychotherapy. In the case of Mr. D., the goal under Behavior is related at the least to those of Affect, Images, and Cognition and may be formulated accurately as "learning mental techniques to relax, think constructively, and organize his time more productively." We shall return to the goals of therapy towards the end of this chapter.

The second model to deal with behavioral patient impairment is the four-level paradigm of Goodman et al. (1992). Under *biopsychology*, the first and core level of functioning, they include both physical manifestations (such as sleep problems, enuresis and encopresis, eating disorders, promiscuity, fire setting, stealing, and hyperactivity, among others) and psychological disturbances (compulsions, delusions, hallucinations, obsessions, paranoia, phobias, dysphoric mood, externalization and blame, dissociative states, grandiosity and psychotic thought, perception, and behavior). Any other psychological symptom listed in the DSM-IV corresponds to the biopsychology level.

Why this long list? Because the presence of any of these symptoms constitutes impairment and warrants mental health care intervention. Unfortunately Goodman et al. do not tell us why they selected the 39 impairments they list in their book (pp. 32–37), though they explain that their choice is based on behavioral manifestations that are "observable and objectifiable" (p. 31). Because of this, a general label such as Depression does not make their list due to its vagueness and behavioral generalization.

The second level of impairment in this model, as indicated above, is that of *intimate relationships*, for which Goodman et al. (1992) list seven impairments. We would like to add the following functional impairments: avoidance of intimacy, noninvolvement/emotional distance, infidelity (emotional, sexual, financial, or a combination), lying and dishonesty, violence, and other observable and objectifiable behaviors related to communication, such as contradicting, arguing about nonsense, put-downs, insults, refusal to praise, lack of kindness, and other such concrete actions. Our list is longer than that of the authors on whom we are commenting.

In the area of *people interaction*, to the 12 impairments listed by Goodman et al. (1992), we add sexual harassment, sexual abuse (including rape in any form), put-downs, lack of praise and kindness, insults, violence, and others.

Finally, at the level of *future orientation*, to the seven impairments listed in the Goodman et al. model, we add unrealistic planning, living beyond one's means, magical thinking (in health, wealth, and relationships), and others.

The great value of Goodman et al.'s presentation is the categorization of impairments within the four areas of human functioning. Their point, as we understand it, is not to give a comprehensive, all-inclusive list of impairments in each area, but rather to emphasize that *mental health care practitioners must always start from concrete, factual, and objective manifestations of dysfunction.* This is the reason their model looks more pathology-oriented than Lazarus' (1981). The specific manifestations of dysfunction must be pinpointed at the onset as belonging to one of the four areas of human functioning.

Unspecified, interpretative and theoretical statements are not accepted to justify treatment, which always should be undertaken only in order to reach a definite goal. This is the only rationale for any psychotherapeutic intervention. Thus, "Patient manifests Oedipal behavior" is unacceptable, while "Withdrawal from interaction with women in the last three months; cancellation of rarely arranged dates with women," describes functional impairment in one who presents the complaint that he cannot find the right person to marry.

Again to use the case of Mr. D. in Chapter 2, his impairment profile, following the Goodman et al. paradigm, would be as follows:

Biopsychology: Violent irritability with wife, altered sleep patterns, muscular tension, erratic habits, restlessness, no regular exercise, inability to concentrate.

Intimacy: Emotionally closed to wife and children, interaction without revealing feelings or responding affectively to others' feelings.

People Interaction: Diminished social contacts with friends and acquaintances, refusal to socialize.

Future Orientation: Worrying about health, money; unable to use his rational mind in order to stop worrying, feeling like a loser with no future worth living for.

If we compare the two models, (see Figures 3.1 and 3.2) Lazarus (1981) and Goodman et al. (1992), we realize that both are useful and comprehensive for the purpose of establishing a profile of the patient's impairment–the P.I.P. of the latter authors. Which each practitioner uses is ultimately a matter of personal preference. Both paradigms are beneficial for the establishment of an objective and comprehensive system for assessing the patient's impairment.

Regardless of the model one chooses, this method of proceeding is not only clinically justified and helpful to the suffering patient, but also convenient for obtaining the necessary authorization or "certification for treatment" from the payers of mental health care.

Incidentally, our criticism of the payers' procedures and policies is reserved for the Conclusion of the book. But in spite of our many objections to the new administration of health care, it makes sense for health insurance companies to know clearly what they are paying for. And to wish for their blind faith in the clinical judgment of the professional is absurd. The mental health care practitioner must learn "the new way" and become adept at considering any patient seeking treatment in terms of functional impairment.

The list of impairments is part of the treatment plan and, because of this, functional impairments not considered as such by the patient are not mentioned in the initial Patient Impairment Profile of Goodman et al. (1992), as, for instance, "Cut off from all relationship with elderly parents due to past ritual abuse in family cult." The patient may have been involved in a family cult and been the victim of sexual abuse many years previously, but the focus of treatment is always the current functional impairment and nothing else. It is true that issues from the past may come up in the course of treatment. For that, however, a new treatment plan will be necessary.

In the treatment plan, only those functional impairments that will be the focus of therapy are listed. Moreover, the impairments

FIGURE 3.1

Patient Impairment Profile

Following the Lazarus (1981) model

	Impairments	Goals of Therapy
Behavior	______	______
Affect	______	______
Sensations	______	______
Images	______	______
Cognition	______	______
Interpersonal	______	______
Diet	______	______

Notes: ______

FIGURE 3.2

Patient Impairment Profile

Following the Goodman, Brown, & Deitz (1992) model

	Impairments	Goals of Therapy
Biopsychology	______	______
Intimacy	______	______
People Interaction	______	______
Future Orientation	______	______

Notes: ______

in the initial list are those for which there is a specific treatment that has a good, research-based chance of correcting them, as we shall discuss in Chapter 6.

To facilitate the practitioner's work, the listing of functional impairments follows one of the two paradigms presented in this chapter, either Goodman et al. (1992) or Lazarus (1981), as explained above. Regarding the treatment plan and the requirement of certification for therapy imposed on practitioners by many managed care companies, either model simplifies with accuracy the description of impairments and the clinical rationale that justifies the treatment proposed.

COMMUNICATING WITH MANAGED CARE COMPANIES

Using once more the case of Mr. D., it would be clear and concise for the managed care corporation to hear over the phone or to read in the initial request for certification of services that the patient is suffering from considerable functional impairments. (We shall deal in Chapter 6 on how to decide on the appropriate treatment.) The question that these companies always ask, at least implicitly, is consistently the same: *Why should we pay for mental health care?* To provide the patient impairment profile is to answer that crucial (and reasonable) question.

If Lazarus' model is followed, Mr. D. needs therapy because he complains of behaviors that did not occur before the psychosocial stressor, namely, inability to concentrate and "to stay put" for more than a few minutes; because he feels insecure, with fears and worries, considering his life worthless; because he is tense, nervous, restless, and unable to get himself to exercise regularly; because of haunting mental pictures of sickness and financial catastrophe that he cannot control; because he has "lost the ability to use his rational thinking"; because his relationship with his wife is angry, tense, and emotionally distant; because with his children and friends, he has become detached and disinterested; because his sleep is erratic due to his worrying, and his meals are irregular.

On the other hand, if the Goodman et al. (1992) model is used, Mr. D.'s need for therapy is also based on his impairments, which, however, are distributed differently, according to the four levels proposed by the authors.

As shown in the clinical case we are using for illustration purposes, the payers of mental health services need to know in every case what the practitioner intends to do or the goals of therapy, which are explained by the patient's inability to control the symptoms that have ensued following retirement, the psychosocial stressor he/she experienced recently. Here, again, the two models provide an orderly way to present the goals of therapy clearly, concisely and concretely.

We stated earlier, at the end of our discussion on Lazarus' paradigm, that the goals of therapy are limited to the disappearance of functional impairments. These goals justify the specific techniques and treatment used. In the case of Mr. D. the goals are listed as follows:

First:	Learn to relax.
Second:	Think constructively.
Third:	Organize his time more productively.
Fourth:	Resume the projects he had planned for his retirement, including regular exercise.
Fifth:	Spend quality time with wife and, through her, resume social contacts.

Because these five gains to be obtained from therapy require that he learn experientially and from within–not merely intellectually–new attitudes and behaviors, Mr. D. will obtain new and real empowerment over his life. For instance, (a) when he starts to worry and to become restless or when he wakes up in the middle of the night, he will possess a new and effective mental tool to handle and control those situations. His (b) greater enjoyment of his wife will make it easier for him to (c) get closer to his children and grandchildren and to (d) renew his social contacts. It is reasonable to hope that this sense of greater self-empowerment will motivate him to increase his social contacts, including his relations with his adult children and young grandchildren.

Even though all this sounds excessive at first hearing, it presents the goals quite logically and progressively. The short-term goals (to be accomplished while he is in treatment) are the five listed above, while the long-term goals are (a) to (d), above, the positive sequelae of treatment.

We emphasize that this way of doing psychotherapy, though

prompted by the vast changes in health care delivery started in the late 1980's and early 1990's, is beneficial to mental health care practitioners. It forces them to be more focused and avoids the hours wasted in irrelevant conversation, often unfairly justified as rapport building or as exploration of inner dynamics.

SUMMARY

This chapter introduces the concept of patient functional impairment as the clinical rationale for psychotherapy. In so doing, we stand in the camp of cognitive behavioral modification, which we prefer to call *cognitive behavioral self-management.* In humans, for things to change effectively, cognition is a *sine qua non*–the "cognitive" in our designation. We also prefer "management" to therapy or even to modification, as in behavior modification, because the concept of self-management conveys more empowerment than either of the other two. We also believe that more emphasis should be placed on the truth that all effective therapy is ultimately self-therapy–what the patient does between sessions with the insights obtained during the therapy session. Because of all of this, we would like to speak simply of self-management or, as one of us has called it, reengineering oneself (Araoz & Sutton, 1994).

The emphasis on coming up with a P.I.P. or patient impairment profile, as Goodman et al. (1992) call it, is a logical one. The practitioner must be very clear about what she/he is asked to help correct, modify, or cancel. The list of impairments is not a vague, theoretical, or interpretative series of concepts (e.g., anal retentive personality traits), but a precise, concrete, measurable definition of behaviors (e.g., extremely possessive of what belongs to her, unwilling to share anything material with others; becomes upset when family or friends "borrow" small things, like ordinary weekly magazines without "asking her permission").

Two models to organize the impairment profile are proposed and the practical application of this method of doing therapy when it comes to dealing with managed care are discussed.

The next chapter, building on this impairment profile, will deal with methods and techniques to reach an accurate diagnosis of Adjustment Disorder.

4

Diagnosis

In establishing a correct diagnosis of Adjustment Disorder, the drawing of a patient impairment profile is one of the most valuable clinical tools. The first question to ask in order to define the problem is: *What has changed in the patient's behavior and become an impairment since the stressful event was experienced?* On the response to this question, the mental health care practitioner can start to formulate the Adjustment Disorder diagnosis. The evidence coming from the initial assessment of impairment provides the rough stuff to determine what is the patient's condition.

Therefore, following the basic question, more information about the patient's condition can be built on it. Thus, the clinician asks: *In what way is the patient's life less productive and enjoyable, less effective and satisfying, as compared to the time before the stressful event took place? Is there evidence of a connection between the current lower level of functioning and the stressful psychosocial occurrence?*

Another important piece of information for the accurate diagnosis of Adjustment Disorder according to DSM-IV relates to the amount of time lapsed since the stressful event took place to the moment when the patient seeks treatment. *How did the patient cope during that period of time? Why is the patient seeking help now?* And, related to this: *What does the patient expect from treatment?*

In outline form, these basic diagnostic inquiries look like this:

1. Psychosocial stressful event, but not extreme nor related to bereavement (DSM-IV, p. 626).
2. Patient impairment: instances and details within three months of the onset of the stressor.

3. Coping *before* the stressor (normal)
   right after the stressor (with some stress)
   currently (with increased difficulty)
4. Patient expects relief from therapy: realistic.
5. Patient commits to therapy.

Adjustment Disorder is a prudent diagnostic choice if these five points coincide: There is an acceptable stressor; there is impairment; there is a deterioration of culturally acceptable coping; there are realistic expectations of therapy; and the patient commits to treatment.

TENTATIVE DIAGNOSIS

At this juncture the practitioner can tentatively diagnose the patient as suffering from Adjustment Disorder. We purposely refer to a *tentative diagnosis* because it takes skill on the part of the diagnostician to identify Adjustment Disorder. For instance, some Personality Disorders produce exaggerated symptoms at the time of stress. This is especially true of the Personality Disorders under Cluster A, whose common symptom is to act in strange and bizarre ways, as we shall discuss in the next chapter. Another area of concern for the differential diagnosis is that of Posttraumatic and/or Acute Stress Disorder, both of which, as DSM-IV (p. 626) warns, also require the occurrence of a psychosocial stressor. The difference is one of degree. Adjustment Disorder can be triggered by a stressor of much less "objective" severity than the one required for Posttraumatic and Acute Stress Disorder.

Obviously, here we stumble into cultural differences: *What constitutes an "objectively" severe or extreme stressor changes from culture to culture.* In case of doubt about the cultural assessment of a stressor, it is imperative to ascertain from relatives and other members of the patient's culture that the patient's reaction to the stressor is, indeed, considered inappropriate and excessive in that culture.

How does the mental health practitioner confirm or reject the initial diagnosis of Adjustment Disorder? One safe way is to check the 10 conditions given by DSM-IV for the differential diagnosis for Adjustment Disorder (p. 625). If there is no evidence of any of these, the diagnosis of Adjustment Disorder stands. The 10 conditions are:

a. Personality Disorders (DSM-IV, p. 629).
b. Mental Retardation (p. 39).
c. Cognition impairment, including memory dysfunction (p. 123).
d. Inability to focus on concrete and specific goals (p. 163).
e. Psychotic symptoms (p. 273 et seq. and p. 317 et seq.).
f. Malingering (p. 683).
g. Substance-Related Disorders (p. 175 et seq.).
h. Age-Related Cognitive Decline (p. 684).
i. Bereavement (p. 684).
j. Religious or spiritual problem (p. 685).

The exclusion of these conditions allows us to think of the impairment presented by the patient in terms of Adjustment Disorder. However, DSM-IV has established six different subtypes of Adjustment Disorder, so that there can be no diagnosis of this condition without specifying its subtype. Therefore, the diagnostician must be familiar with the following six subtypes:

309.0 Adjustment Disorder with Depressed Mood

This diagnosis is used when the stressor has produced impairment in the patient with *predominant manifestations* of feeling down and depressed, with feelings of hopelessness and unhappiness, with tearfulness, and uncontrollable bouts of crying that interfere with normal (prestressor) functioning.

309.24 Adjustment Disorder with Anxiety

This is the diagnosis to use when the main symptoms of impairment are nervousness, general apprehension, worrying, inability to stop one's thoughts of doom and negativism, jitteriness, and irritability while the patient wonders why she/he is "out of control" regarding these symptoms, yet realizes intellectually that the symptoms are irrational. In children, the same diagnosis is correct if, since the stressful event, they have developed a new fear of separation from important persons in their life, for instance, refusing to sleep alone, to go to school, or even to be in another room away from an important attachment figure.

309.28 Adjustment Disorder with Mixed Anxiety and Depressed Mood

This diagnostic subtype is used when the patient exhibits a combination of symptoms from the previous two subtypes and his/her life is mostly dominated by these symptoms. Daily functioning is truly impaired because the patient does not find the resources in the self to stop these feelings and to go on with the chores and concerns of normal living.

309.3 Adjustment Disorder with Disturbance of Conduct

Some patients react to a psychosocial stressor with noticeable change in behavior, such as shoplifting, drunkenness, getting into fights, breaking rules they usually did not break before, becoming overly aggressive, not paying bills, lying, becoming annoyingly flirtatious or promiscuous, using drugs or reverting to heavy cigarette smoking after many years of abstinence, losing interest in sex, or sleeping much less or more than their norm. A curious feature is that the patients do not show much concern, guilt, or remorse for their unusual behavior. In all these cases this diagnosis is in order.

309.4 Adjustment Disorder with Mixed Disturbance of Emotions and Conduct

Other patients engage in the same disturbed behavior and also show emotional symptoms, repenting and blaming themselves for their uncommon conduct, merely to revert to it shortly thereafter. Or they feel anxious and fearful after having done something illegal, dangerous, or otherwise unacceptable, only to repeat the same behavior in the near future. This diagnosis identifies these patients correctly.

309.9 Adjustment Disorder Unspecified

When the reaction to a stressful psychosocial event does not fall into any of the categories covered by the five previous subtypes, DSM-IV provides the practitioner with this "catch all" subtype. Many patients develop physical complaints, often serious and life-threatening, shortly after a serious psychosocial event. History tells us, for instance, that Marie Antoinette became completely gray-haired overnight when she was imprisoned during the popular revolution that created the French Republic.

This diagnosis also has a broader scope. It is used when persons show considerable changes, usually for worse, in work or academic functioning without exhibiting emotions either of anxiety or depression in any of its forms. They may withdraw from human contacts, not answering letters or phone calls, spending much time alone (behaviors that are unusual for them), and responding to queries about this conduct with general statements such as, "I don't feel like it," meaning that they have lost interest in interacting with people with whom they usually interacted in the past. Obviously this is not the type of behavior referred to in the subtype "with disturbance of conduct," above, but it is still unusual for this particular individual.

Another example of the exaggerated behavior mode is the person who, after experiencing a psychosocial stressor, engages in exorbitant amounts of work, to the point that he/she becomes exhausted or sick and the patient or his/her family seek therapy. The subtype, "unspecified," as can be seen, provides the diagnostician with a place for these and many more functional impairments not specified in the first five subtypes of Adjustment Disorder.

All these six subtypes of Adjustment Disorder remind us of the functional meaning of symptoms. They are developed as coping strategies, but prove to be maladaptive and not infrequently dysfunctional and even self-destructive. If the symptom is a metaphor representing a unique inner experience, we may do well to remember that all these symptoms are attempts at surviving, physically and mentally, in the face of a change that has derailed life.

To determine what diagnostic subtype of Adjustment Disorder is appropriate for a particular patient the following checklist (Figure 4.1) may be useful.

FIGURE 4.1

General Checklist for Adjustment Disorders

Directions: Check as many as apply. The more checks on the two right columns ("Often," "Much") the more accurate is the AD diagnosis.

KEY
N=Never
S =Somewhat
O=Often
M=Much

	N	S	O	M
1. Thinks of stressor				
2. Wastes time with the thought				
3. Depressed				
4. Tearful				
5. Hopeless				
6. Nervous				
7. Worrying				
8. Jittery or other physical symptom (specify)				
9. Angry				
10. More dependent TBS (Than Before Stressor)				
11. Ambivalent				
12. Truancy				
13. Vandalism				
14. Reckless driving				
15. Fighting				
16. Defaulting in legal responsibilities				
17. Poorer work performance TBS				
18. Poorer academic performance TBS				
19. Less concentration TBS				
20. Withdraws from social activities				
21. Avoids people				
22. Avoids fun activities				

NOTES FOR GENERAL CHECKLIST

Responses of patients to the General Checklist for Adjustment Disorders lead to one of the six specific categories of DSM-IV. Because there is no diagnosis of Adjustment Disorder without a specific subtype, the responses of the General Checklist must be elucidated.

309.0 Adjustment Disorder with Depressed Mood

"Often" and "Much" responses to Nos. 1, 3, 4, 5, 9, 11, 20, and 22 elicit the following *or similar* follow-up questions:

1. What happens to you physically when you feel depressed?
2. What events, thoughts, or people make you tearful?
3. How do you describe your feeling hopeless?
4. When do you feel especially angry?
5. How do you describe your ambivalence?
6. From what social activities have you withdrawn lately?
7. What fun activities have you avoided?
8. When do you think of stressor more often or intensely?

309.24 Adjustment Disorder with Anxiety

"Often" and "Much" responses to Nos. 1, 5, 6, 7, 8, 17 or 18, and 19 elicit these or similar follow-up questions:

1. When is your hopelessness worse?
2. How do you cope with it?
3. How do you experience your nervousness?
4. What do you worry about?
5. What do you do about your physical symptoms?
6. How has this (what you do to cope) helped you?
7. Give details of the changes in your activities.
8. How are you not able to concentrate as before?
9. When do you specifically think more of the stressor?
10. What happens then? (e.g., "I become anxious")
11. What do you do then? (coping strategies)

309.28 Adjustment Disorder with Mixed Anxiety and Depressed Mood

The diagnosis for this subtype is based on a combination of the two previous subtypes. Consequently, the same follow-up questions are used in this case when the responses to Nos. 1, 3, 4, 5, 6, 7, 8, 9, 10, 11, 17, 18, 19, 20, and 22 fall under "Often" or "Much."

309.3 Adjustment Disorder with Disturbance of Conduct

The following *or similar* follow-up questions are used when "Often" and "Much" responses are given to questions Nos. 12, 13, 14, 15, and 16 in the General Checklist.

1. What triggers your (specific) conduct?
2. What goes through your mind, if anything, before you decide to do or engage in ______?
3. Do you think that you could stop yourself from doing ______?
4. What reasons do you use in your thinking *not* to stop?
5. Why do you want to change this (conduct) now by coming for treatment?
6. How do you explain that you end up doing what you don't want to do?

309.4 Adjustment Disorder with Mixed Disturbance of Emotions and Conduct

This subtype, like 309.28, is also a combination of previous ones, namely, 309.0, 309.24, and 309.3. Therefore, the follow-up questions suggested under those three categories apply here, too.

309.9 Adjustment Disorder Unspecified

When 10 or more answers in the General Checklist fall under "Never" or "Somewhat" and Nos. 8, 16, 17, 18, 20, and 21 fall under "Often" and/or "Much" the diagnosis belongs to this subtype.

DIAGNOSTIC VIGNETTES

Before proceeding, the following four diagnostic vignettes may be of help to the practitioner in the differential diagnosis of Adjustment Disorder. These vignettes provide an opportunity to test one's skills by determining a specific diagnostic subtype of Adjustment Disorder for each of these four clinical cases. The correct diagnoses with their rationale will be found at the end of the chapter.

Case #1: Marc

Marc, a 54-year-old married airline engineer, had to choose between moving from Chicago to Atlanta or quitting his job with a large airline and losing his retirement pension. He moved alone to Georgia and traveled home to his wife on Friday evenings to return to his office on Sunday night. During the first six or seven weeks, he didn't mind doing this and his wife, a very positive personality, supported Marc to the hilt and talked to him over the telephone frequently.

However, during the second month she realized that her husband of almost 30 years, who had never before abused alcohol, was often intoxicated when they spoke by telephone. She also found evidence of his having some special relationship with a woman who worked for the same airline, something he had never done before in the marriage.

When she brought this up during a weekend, he became very anxious and defensive. Later that Sunday, he left for Atlanta five hours earlier than his regularly scheduled flight, informing her of his decision to leave early as he left the house. Later that same night, when his wife called him over the phone, he sounded very drunk and very depressed. The conversation was brief and he focused on his "crazy life, without a home, working like a slave." The wife called him back early Monday morning before he left for work. Marc was not drunk now, but still sounded very depressed and kept reassuring himself and his wife of their mutual love.

That weekend was a turning point. The wife insisted on Marc seeing a physician. He refused. She took a two-week leave of absence from her job and flew to Atlanta, saying that she would not return home until he had seen a mental health care practitioner. He gave in and made an appointment with a Counseling Psychologist, who saw him with his wife twice and alone two more times before his wife went back to Chicago.

What diagnosis did the Counseling Psychologist formulate for Marc? The answer is to be found at the end of this chapter. However, as we suggested before, the reader should make an effort to establish a precise diagnosis, recognizing all the reasons leading to a decision on a particular category.

Case #2: Elizabeth

Elizabeth is a 40-year-old married woman, enrolled in a doctoral program in clinical psychology. Throughout her life she has experienced periods of low self-esteem, followed by general lethargy, but was always in excellent health and very seldom had any mild physical symptoms.

Five months before, she had taken a leave of absence from her job in academia in order to complete her clinical internship. Subsequently, she learned that her job would not be available to her, as was previously agreed upon before she took her leave of absence. Although she had a very positive experience with her internship, she was still two years away from completing her doctoral degree. The change in the couple's financial situation due to her separation from a good paying job, added to the normal but heavy pressures of her internship in a ghetto psychiatric hospital, created exceptional stress in the marriage. She developed frequent headaches and severe stomach cramps that her physician was not able to diagnose medically. She felt depleted of energy at night when she returned home from her internship and often fell asleep right after dinner.

Her husband, although supportive of her educational pursuits, started to resent their inability to spend meaningful time together and tension escalated between them, with emotional distance, sarcasm, and infrequent sexual encounters. She told her friends that she felt emotionally empty and sick to her stomach.

Her clinical supervisor complained that her work was not as good as it was at the beginning of the internship and advised her to "go into therapy in order to get herself together." Elizabeth visited a Family Psychologist who told her what she believed to be her diagnosis. Before looking up the correct answer at the end of the chapter, please, decide what diagnosis you would assign Elizabeth and go over your rationale for your choice in as much detail as you can.

Case #3: Ed

At 39, Ed is an office manager who has been involved in a homosexual relationship for the past four years. However, this relationship has become estranged in the last two months due to his lover's desire to date other men without leaving Ed. Prior to this liaison, Ed was married for two years, but because his ex-wife wanted to return to her country of origin, they decided to divorce, as he had no intention of living in a foreign country. Although he was not unhappy in his marriage, he felt more comfortable in the current relationship, which had lasted longer than his marriage.

When asked about his life style, he stated that he was relatively happy, but that in the last two months he often felt anxious and depressed about the choice of a same-sex relationship he had made and how it might affect his future. He felt that there were some issues he still needed to resolve like getting married and having children. Therefore, he was not sure whether he should continue in this relationship, leading an alternate lifestyle. He felt anxious about turning 40 and reported that he woke up in the middle of the night worrying about his life. Because Ed had been in therapy before to resolve issues related to his family background (both parents were alcoholics), he decided to return to therapy to discuss his present dilemma.

The therapist, a Clinical Psychologist, suggested couple therapy and Ed assured her that his lover had already decided to go ahead with what he wanted and said there was nothing to talk about in therapy. With this, she agreed to see Ed individually. What diagnosis did the psychologist assign Ed? Go over the case once more, if necessary, and formulate your own diagnosis for Ed before you read the diagnostic rationale at the conclusion of the chapter.

Case #4: Lucy

Lucy, 26 years old, moved four months ago from Milwaukee to New York City with her husband of three years. Both she and her husband wanted to experience life in the big city. Neither had jobs in New York before leaving their hometown, but both managed to find work with a temporary agency.

After two months in New York, her husband met another woman and began seeing her. He covered up his affair with the excuse that he had to work overtime. After a few weeks, Lucy became aware of his relationship with the other woman and moved out. She was now living alone as she felt she needed time to sort things out. Her husband kept telling her that he loved her and promised to stop the liaison with his mistress, but she was still very frightened of moving back in with her husband.

Recently, she began experiencing difficulties falling asleep and was tense and nervous in general. She had become afraid of staying in the apartment alone and was frightened of noises that she heard at night. She found herself biting her fingernails and constantly talking to co-workers about her situation. Without conviction, she said her self-disclosure was needed to get things off her chest and that her lack of friends in New York City forced her to talk to her co-workers, the only people who knew her.

One of her co-workers related to her that she had a similar problem with her boyfriend and was now going to therapy to make changes in her life. She told Lucy how therapy had helped her focus on the positive aspects of her life and encouraged Lucy to see a therapist.

DIAGNOSES FOR THE PREVIOUS CLINICAL CASES

Case # 1: Marc

Diagnosis: Adjustment Disorder with Mixed Disturbance of Emotions and Conduct (309.4).
Rationale: The psychosocial stressor–being forced by economic circumstances to move alone to another city with which the pa-

tient was not familiar–altered his whole lifestyle. There is no evidence of any of the 10 conditions listed earlier in this chapter in order to check on the accuracy of the Adjustment Disorder diagnosis which is the third criterion of DSM-IV for Adjustment Disorder.

No precedent for his "disturbance of emotions and conduct" was detected in Marc's past. The functional impairment began within two months from his move to a new city (first criterion in DSM-IV for this condition). The impairment symptoms are clinically significant, such as drinking and intimacy with another woman (DSM-IV, second criterion). There is no bereavement present (fourth criterion), and there is good expectation that the symptoms will disappear with the help of brief psychotherapy, according to Betz (1987) and Hays & Oxley (1986), which is the fifth criterion of DSM-IV for Adjustment Disorder.

Case #2: Elizabeth

Diagnosis: Adjustment Disorder Unspecified (309.9).
Rationale: The patient clearly expressed physical symptoms such as headaches and stomach cramps. These symptoms have been ruled out medically. The onset of these physical manifestations was brought about after the patient became aware of the potential loss of her job–the identified psychosocial stressor. Prior to that event, there were no indications of unusual stressors. General lethargy and low energy were also experienced as a physical manifestation in this case, and there was evidence of tension in her marriage and diminished job performance.

The symptoms began within the three months time frame required by the DSM-IV diagnostic category for Adjustment Disorder. The diagnosis of Somatization Disorder (300.81) is excluded because the physical symptoms started at the age of 40.

In view of all this and because the five DSM-IV criteria for all Adjustment Disorders mentioned in the diagnosis of the first case (Marc) apply here too, other Adjustment Disorder subtypes are excluded. Because the old (DSM-III-R) subtype "Adjustment Disorder with Physical Complaints" does not appear in DSM-IV, the

"Unspecified" subtype must be used in the case of Elizabeth, whose maladaptive reactions include serious physical symptoms.

Case #3: Ed

Diagnosis: Adjustment Disorder with Mixed Anxiety and Depressed Mood (309. 28).
Rationale: This subtype combines symptoms found in both Adjustment Disorder with Anxiety and Adjustment Disorder with Depressed Mood, accompanied by feelings of decreased self-esteem and worthlessness.

The fact that Ed reports often feeling anxious and depressed, awakening in the middle of the night and thinking morosely about his life, is indicative of the predominant features associated with depression. The confusion about his homosexual lifestyle and the preoccupation about his future with the choices he has in order to make decisions underlie issues of poor self-esteem.

These issues have become more apparent to him as he approaches 40, a significant developmental step, coupled with the new estrangement between him and his lover. Both these events are the psychosocial stressors that have manifested themselves at this time in his life.

Since there are no indications of other mental disorders and all the criteria for this diagnosis are fulfilled (see the first case of Marc), the Adjustment Disorder subtype with Mixed Anxiety and Depressed Mood is the most appropriate for Ed's case.

Case #4: Lucy

Diagnosis: Adjustment Disorder with Anxiety (309.24).
Rationale: The essential features of the subtype, Adjustment Disorder with Anxiety, are symptoms such as nervousness, worry, and sleep disturbances. Lucy reports nail biting, which is a common external manifestation of nervousness. She feels compelled to keep talking to her co-workers about her problem, even though this is against her better judgment–another indication of anxiety. These symptoms appeared after the estrangement from her husband and

her starting to live alone, both occurring approximately two months after her arrival in New York City.

First, there is no evidence of any other mental disorders, such as Obsessive-Compulsive Personality Disorder (301.4) or Borderline Personality Disorder (301.83). Second, Lucy's functional impairment was brought about by her husband's unfaithfulness–the psychosocial stressor. Third, the five criteria for Adjustment Disorder are present (see Marc's case, above). Therefore, the appropriate diagnosis for Lucy is that of Adjustment Disorder with Anxiety.

In the next chapter, special attention will be given to Personality Disorders in order to make sure the diagnosis is correct.

5

Adjustment and Personality

Of the 10 exclusionary conditions summarized from DSM-IV, p. 625, and listed early in the last chapter, Personality Disorders are the most sensitive. This is the reason for this brief discussion here. Unlike in Chapter 3 on patient impairment, an adaptation of only one model is presented here because it follows the DSM-III-R (1987) and DSM-IV (1994) classification of Personality Disorders.

In dealing with Personality Disorders, DSM-IV reminds us (p. 633) that its approach is *categorical* as contrasted with *dimensional*. The categorical perspective states that if a person exhibits certain behaviors, s/he falls under a specific category that "represent(s) qualitatively distinct clinical syndromes" (p. 633). Thus, *odd or eccentric behavior*, under Cluster A of Personality Disorders (p. 634), "categorizes" the Paranoid, Schizoid, and Schizotypal Personality Disorders. Next, *dramatic and emotional self-centeredness*, under Cluster B, gives us the categories of Antisocial, Borderline, Histrionic, and Narcissistic Personality Disorders. Finally, *anxious or fearful behavior*, under Cluster C, establishes the categories of Avoidant, Dependent, and Obsessive-Compulsive Personality Disorders.

From a clinical viewpoint, however, the dimensional approach is more practical because the diagnostician is seldom faced with clear-cut behaviors in patients. Most times, there is a mixture of symptoms or a lack of clarity as to the duration of them. This is an important point given the fact that DSM-IV Personality Disorder diagnoses always include a time frame: early childhood for Cluster A, and early adulthood for Clusters B and C, except the Antisocial Personality Disorder, specifically "occurring since age 15 years" (DSM-IV, p. 649).

DSM-IV decided against the dimensional approach because there is still much to be learned about the progression of personality traits, indeed about the traits themselves. But the clinician finds it useful to know what has been the personality style (the "M.O." or modus operandi) of a patient. In order to facilitate the inquiry into a patient's habitual manner of acting, we have built a model on the groundbreaking work by Oldham & Morris (1990) on which we base our *Personality Profile*, which follows the dimensional perspective.

If one is in doubt about the patient's personality, especially about where to draw the line between style and disorder, it is helpful to establish a personality profile. If the patient has exhibited marked signs of a personality style in the past, his/her adjustment impairment must be viewed in that context. On the other hand, if s/he is exhibiting extreme symptoms since the occurrence of a stressful psychosocial event in his/her life, the stressor is assumed to have exacerbated a previously covert personality disorder that now manifests itself under stress.

The criteria necessary to decide on the 10 DSM-IV Personality Disorders are readily available in that publication (p. 633). We remind the reader that what ends in a Personality Disorder *may* have started as a personality style exhibiting one rather noticeable trait throughout the patient's life that friends and family perceived as an idiosyncrasy of the person. "That's the way s/he is," is the frequent comment with a shrug of the shoulders. Only when the person becomes functionally impaired because of that idiosyncrasy do friends and family admit that that peculiar trait was excessive.

The following list of excessive/dominant personality traits (Table 5.1) that *may* prepare the way for a personality disorder is adapted from Oldham & Morris (1990).

We believe that an *excessive* trait must be present in a patient in order for the clinician to be concerned about a possible Personality Disorder. What constitutes an excessive trait depends largely on cultural considerations. It is also useful to remember that all normal people exhibit in mild or moderate form a combination of many of the personality traits listed above. Finally, it must be emphasized that cultural and ethnic variables enter into the picture. Some personality traits are considered important virtues in many cultures and a knowledge of the patient's cultural values is essential for one

TABLE 5.1

Excessive/Dominant Personality Traits

Trait	Disorder
Cluster A (eccentricity)	
Careful	Paranoid
Loner	Schizoid
Peculiar	Schizotypal
Cluster B (self-centeredness)	
Nonconformist	Antisocial
Unpredictable	Borderline
Overreactive	Histrionic
Self-assured	Narcissistic
Cluster C (anxiety)	
Compassionate	Avoidant
Dedicated	Dependent
Responsible	Obsessive-Compulsive

to determine accurately to what extent a specific personality trait is a positive or negative variable in the diagnostic profile of the patient.

A brief description of how each dominant personality trait colors one's whole individuality is in order.

The *careful* person is one who has been and is always attentive, on guard, alert to all the messages and information that come from the outside.

Loners prefer to be by themselves. They don't need people. Others' reactions to them do not matter. They are detached and, perhaps because of this trait, often have great insights into human nature in general and individuals in particular.

Peculiar people are noticed because they are "different" in their dress, demeanor, tastes. Many geniuses in various fields have this excessive trait, but not all those who have it *are* geniuses.

Nonconformists are rebels. Just because everyone else does a thing one way, they do it differently, often annoying others. Rules and laws are challenges perceived to be broken, evaded, or ignored. They often use the fast lane, always on the edge, taking risks even when there is no need to do so.

The *unpredictable* are intense in love and hate, jumping into situations, relationships, and changes just for the thrill of it. For them, life is full of ups and downs, glory and hell, and they cannot feel alive without constant emotional turmoil.

Overeactives are very sensitive, generous, kind, and understanding, and often expect others to be likewise. They color all experiences with emotion and pathos, which they express all the time in sublime art, in humor, in sensuality, and even in violence.

Self-assured people are leaders and even when small in size have an imposing presence. They are looked up to by others who depend on their ambition and vision to make their own dreams come true. They "sell" their ideas with skill even to large, difficult crowds and use clever schemes to gain further influence and power.

The *compassionate* deal best with a small group in which they flourish and in which they hide from popularity. But here they become pillars and rocks on which the others depend for inspiration, support, and validation.

The *dedicated* know commitment and loyalty, always helping others. Their dedication gives meaning to their existence; they truly experience and feel that in giving they are rewarded.

Responsible people worship exactitude, duty, rules, and tradition. A strong sense of morality gives them certitude and security. Fun often means to get the job done even though it requires the sacrifice of sleep and meals and of what most mortals consider fun, like play, socializing, and so on.

These brief descriptions are useful to establish a *Personality Profile* when the clinician has reason to be apprehensive about a possible Personality Disorder. In this case, the form provided (Figure 5.1) may be convenient. This form is a modified adaptation of Oldham

FIGURE 5.1

Personality Profile

Directions: Score patient on the 7-point scale (1= very few, if any, indications of this trait; 7=many signs of this trait; 4=average). Join the scores of all 10 traits with a straight line. The right side skew of the profile will provide an indication of the personality disorder.

PATIENT'S NAME ______________________ DATE ________

Trait	**1**	**2**	**3**	**4**	**5**	**6**	**7**	**Disorder**
Careful								Paranoid
Loner								Schizoid
Peculiar								Schizothymic
Nonconformist								Antisocial
Unpredictable								Borderline
Overreacting								Histrionic
Self-assured								Narcissistic
Compassionate								Avoidant
Dedicated								Dependent
Responsible								Obsessive-Compulsive
	1	**2**	**3**	**4**	**5**	**6**	**7**	

NOTES: ____

____

& Morris (1990, p. 21), although they do not use a Personality Profile as such, but rather a Personality Self-Portrait Graph. What we offer is a convenient tool to summarize information gathered during the diagnostic interview in order to help the clinician in the formulation of an accurate diagnosis.

When one is interpreting the results of this assessment, the Personality Profile is revealing. The more that scores fall on the right hand side, the greater the possibility of a Personality Disturbance. If this happens, a thorough clinical personality evaluation is in order so as to be sure that what appeared as an Adjustment Disorder is not an indication of Personality Disturbance.

Alternately, the more scores fall on the left hand side, the greater reason there is to proceed with the Adjustment Disorder diagnosis without further concern about the possible presence of a Personality Disorder.

To familiarize the mental health practitioner with this delicate area of Adjustment Disorder diagnosis, we offer four clinical vignettes, in the same style of the previous chapter, asking the reader to decide on the type of diagnosis that is appropriate for each case before reading the answer at the end of the chapter.

CLINICAL VIGNETTES

Case #1: Mrs. May

At 78, Mrs. May requested therapy, complaining that her three daughters and one son were conspiring to put her away in a nursing home. Wealthy, bright, educated, and well traveled, she lived with a cook and butler in a large mansion appraised at over five million dollars. Her physical health was excellent, thanks, in part, to her hygienic habits and regular exercise. "There is no reason in the world to force me to change my lifestyle," she emphasized. Detailed exploration showed that Mrs. May was perfectly able to continue living alone and that she was completely coherent without any indications of Age-Related Cognitive Decline (DSM-IV # 780.9). "This has been going on for three years and I can't get through to them. And now they want to take action." She added, "I've begged them to come to family therapy in order to discuss this, but they refuse and treat me as if I were senile. They want to destroy me. They know I'd never adjust to living in a nursing home."

Because of her children's recent threat, she had, unbeknownst to them, hired a prestigious law firm in order to fight their efforts to place her in a nursing home. Before proceeding to the whole extent of legal action, she was trying to get the whole family together and avoid the ill feelings that legal action would no doubt produce.

She came to therapy to discuss this and to check if the therapist could be instrumental in making this family meeting possible. She made it clear that her interest in avoiding a family feud was to protect the family name as well as the grandchildren and their offspring, not her own children. She was intent on hurting them if they did not drop their plans and, in her words, "putting them in the poorhouse, if need be. To me they are strangers now, and they deserve all the pain and grief I can inflict on them."

Mrs. May was reacting to her psychosocial stressful event by taking action, but feeling, at the same time, strong emotions that she found to be "new" and difficult to manage. In spite of her external composure and dignity, she was obviously upset and very ambivalent about proceeding with legal action against her children.

In order to explain her understanding of the children's decision to "dump (her) in a nursing home," she mentioned that the son was running for political office with the full support of the three daughters. Now she was an embarrassment to them because she had always been "a rebel" in the midst of a distinguished and traditional New England family. Zen, atheism, and nudism were causes she supported wholeheartedly with finances and active participation. Not the type of popular interests usually seen in a conservative New England community.

She seemed to enjoy shocking people. Her lifestyle was also flamboyant and "different." She drove a red convertible Ferrari at high speed, dressed unconventionally for a lady her age, and used teenage language. Her grandchildren (30 and 24) and the three great grandchildren adored and admired her, but her own children–conservative, middle-aged, businesspeople with political connections and well known in the community–had always been trying to change her ways and "make me as dull and insipid as they are," she explained. This was especially so since her husband's death three years previously. When he was alive, he protected her from the community gossips and from the children's criticism, acting as a peacemaker between them and their mother. As a very successful businessman, owner of much valuable real estate in New York City, Philadelphia, and Boston, he had provided extremely well for the family and left Mrs. May financially very comfortable.

Now that the son was a candidate for political office, the children wanted the world to forget that this colorful lady was their mother. A nursing home seemed a good place to keep her away from the public eye and to suggest that many of her antics had been due to her senility, from which she now needed protection by her children.

The therapist contacted the oldest daughter, as the mother had requested, in order to suggest a family meeting. Not only did the daughter refuse to have such meeting, but she indicated that the mother's going to a therapist was a clear indication of her paranoia and accused the clinician of taking advantage of "a demented old lady" in order to benefit from her money. The conversation confirmed much of Mrs. May's story.

Case #2: Michael

While no one was at home, a gas explosion had destroyed Michael's house where he lived with his wife and two-year-old son. He used to dislike that house because it was dark, decaying, and depressing, as he described it. He had considered the destruction of his house a blessing in disguise. Because the house was run down, it needed constant attention and repair, an expensive and time-consuming annoyance for him. The insurance money had come much sooner than expected, and the family had moved into the new house only two months ago. The new house was modern and beautiful and Michael had fixed a small room in it as his studio where he had his own computer, his books, and his work desk.

His wife loved the new place, more modern, bigger, and in a better location than the old house. All the excitement and commotion of moving and fixing the new home had given her renewed energy and joy. But Michael, busy with all the details of establishing their home, buying furniture, deciding on wallpaper and paint colors, etc., started to feel restless, unhappy, unable to sleep well, distracted and unable to control his appetite. Much as he liked the idea of a new house and his own private studio, now that they had moved in to the new house, he felt he wanted to be in the old house. He sensed that he could not adjust to the new place and felt miserable inside.

Michael's father was a psychotherapist with whom Michael had always had a good relationship, calling him on the phone about once a week and seeing him once or twice a month. Now Michael found himself calling him practically every day. Michael also realized that he had become overly attached to his wife, needing her advice to select his clothes to go to work, to decide whether to take the car to the car wash, to make up his mind to call his father. He could not make the simplest decision without asking her, as if he needed her permission or blessing for everything. He was never sure of himself.

His wife, a financial consultant, had to travel once or twice a month, staying in another city one or two nights at a time. He always had depended on her for many things, believing this was a sign of a close marriage, but now he felt fearful and helpless when he was alone with his son on the nights when she was away. As a matter of fact, during her last trip–two nights away from home–he had been unable to sleep alone and found excuses to have his son sleep in the same bed with him. He realized that "something was wrong with (him)" and wanted to "change back to (his) old self," to quote him.

Case #3: Ann

A former model and dancer, Ann, 31, had been in a serious car accident which left her walking with a noticeable limp after surgery. With several months of physical therapy, she still was not able to work as she did before the accident, even though the physical therapist assured her that conditions like hers took time for full recovery and that the prognosis was excellent for complete cure.

When she sought psychotherapy, about 10 weeks after the accident, she confessed that she had entertained suicidal thoughts a few weeks back. She was ashamed of these thoughts because she, as a devout Catholic, considered these thoughts sinful. What stopped the negative thinking was the interest that an old high school sweetheart, recently divorced, had started to show in her. She was very happy with this budding relationship and wanted to have a more positive attitude about her recovery and to stop constantly questioning her physical therapist in her mind. She knew that she had one of the most competent and experienced physical therapists in the area, but she kept doubting his reassurances and treatment.

She described herself, on the one hand, checking carefully and often condemning in her mind everything the physical therapist said and did, both professionally and in relation to her as an attractive woman, and, on the other hand, going through mental torture every day when she practiced the exercises prescribed for her rehabilitation. Instead of spending half an hour a day doing the exercises, she spent at times up to three hours in order to make sure she did them right, moralistically condemning herself for being negligent. Because of this concern with doing exactly what the therapist prescribed, she had lost interest in every other facet of her life, including most friendships.

Asked about the professional conduct of the physical therapist, she could not pinpoint any instance of even the semblance of malpractice on his part. She simply said, "You know, he sees me practically naked and as a man he has to react. But that is sinful and wrong."

However, with her new beau, she was questioning his motivation "in being attracted to a cripple," to repeat her expression, as if his only incentive must be her money.

Questioned about this tendency to doubt everything, Ann responded poignantly; "Well, I guess this is part of my compulsivity. How do you think I became a dancer? You could never be a dancer if you are not a perfectionist. The slightest little detail makes a big difference. But that's the way I've been since I was a little girl. I'm ashamed to tell you this, but my mother told me that I was impossible about cleanliness, even as an infant; that I always kept asking her when she gave me a bath, you know, I always bothered her: Are my ears clean? Is my back clean? Did she soap my neck good enough, you know?"

Now, the fact that Anne was unable to walk perfectly triggered the same perfectionistic tendency. She said, "I know this is silly but I cannot stop my thoughts and I need you to teach me how to stop this nonsense."

Case #4: Max

Max, 45, a professor of English Literature at a large university, came into therapy three months after he had been informed that his teaching position had been terminated. He was single, stated that he wanted to get married, but had a long list of conditions for the right mate. He spent most of his free time alone, taking care of his fish tank, his three Chihuahua dogs, and his expensive sports car. His life had been quiet, uneventful, and routinized, with very few friends, little traveling, and marginal involvement in professional or community activities. His family, married sister and brother with their children, lived in another state, and he saw them only once a year for the Christmas holidays.

Now he felt devastated. The order of his life had been disrupted, and he was angry ("After all the work I did there!"), refusing to look actively for another position in the academic community. He stated repeatedly that he had never expected to be fired, that this was an injustice, that he had consulted with a lawyer of the Professor's Union and had been told there was nothing he could do because he had no permanent contract and that he was going to get himself a really good lawyer though he did not think he could afford one.

All his life, Max had taken the safe road, not wanting conflict of any kind, not taking risks, and not making waves, even in his professional writings, which were only two articles. Though the publication of scholarly writings was expected of him as a professor, he was still working on a historical research book 10 years after he had started it because he believed that it was not good enough for publication. One of the reasons given for his termination as a professor was his lack of scholarly publications. However, he was excellent as a teacher, though aloof and detached, with the reputation of being a rather unfriendly intellectual.

When he consulted a mental health professional, he still had a whole semester to find another academic appointment. However, as in the case of his ideal mate, he had a list of conditions. One of them was that he did not want to move away from the New York metropolitan area even though he took little advantage of the cultural opportunities that the city offered. He visited a museum and went to the theatre on an average of once a year.

The clinician encouraged Max to ready his massive manuscript for publication since two prestigious publishers had shown interest in his historical research. Max countered that at this time he was too upset to concentrate on that task and too distracted with his search for a top lawyer (whom he could not afford) to be able to do anything about his book.

Before checking the correct diagnosis for each of the four vignettes you just read, keep in mind that often what is presented as a problem of adjustment hides an additional Personality Disorder. For the benefit of the patient, both issues must be addressed in most cases. Managed care companies must be informed of this situation and must be educated about these special cases. We believe that it is unethical to ignore Axis II in cases such as those just presented.

By dealing only with the Adjustment Disorder, a mental health care practitioner is as negligent as the physician who, discovering high blood pressure in a patient who has come for another medical condition, treats the latter without doing anything about the high blood pressure.

The clinician must inform the managed care organization about the Axis II diagnosis, explaining the need for additional therapy sessions in order to treat the Personality Disorder, which often is at the root of the maladaptive reaction to the psychosocial stressor responsible for the patient's functional impairment.

DIAGNOSES FOR THE CLINICAL VIGNETTES

Case #1: Mrs. May

Diagnosis: Axis I: Adjustment Disorder with Anxiety (309.24) and Parent-Child Relational Problem (V61. 20).
Axis II: Diagnosis Deferred (799.9).

Rationale: Mrs. May is reacting to the threat of a drastic change in her lifestyle forced upon her by the adult children. She is rationally doing all in her power to impede this: legal action, attempts to get the children together in order to discuss the situation, consulting a therapist.

Because the psychosocial stressor continues, her condition cannot be diagnosed as Posttraumatic Stress Disorder (309.81). Neither is Generalized Anxiety Disorder (308.02) a correct diagnosis because the patient continues to function appropriately in all areas of her life. Therefore, on Axis I, a rather descriptive statement (V61.20) serves the diagnostic need and specifies the source of the anxiety in the Adjustment Disorder.

However, on Axis II, the deferred diagnosis serves to explain some of the symptoms that may be otherwise misleading. Mrs. May's disregard for what is conventional and culture-appropriate and her desire to hurt the children whom she regards now as strangers could be interpreted as indications of Antisocial Personality Disorder (301.7). Her rather flamboyant lifestyle could be seen as belonging to the Histrionic Personality Disorder (301.50). The combination of these features could be used to establish the diagnosis of Personality Disorder NOS (301.9). However, the idiosyncratic behavior of Mrs. May does not necessarily betray a Personality *Disorder* and for that reason, we prefer to defer the diagnosis in Axis II.

Case #2: Michael

Diagnosis: Axis I: Adjustment Disorder with Anxiety (309.24).
Axis II: Dependent Personality Disorder (301.6).

Rationale: Because the functional impairment started as a consequence of the old house being destroyed and of moving into the new house, there is justification to use the diagnosis of Adjustment Disorder. Since Michael shows definite signs of anxiety, that subtype was chosen.

Even though Michael considered the destruction of the old house as a blessing in disguise, as he said, the symptoms he described indicated the presence of Adjustment Disorder. Moreover, the stressor–the house blowing up due to a gas explosion–activated in him a, thus far, latent Dependent Personality Disorder, which had been masked in the marriage by great closeness with his wife and in the relationship with his father, whom he treated as a close friend. Both these interactions had escalated since the house explosion, making overt the existence of a Dependent Personality Disorder.

But, why not diagnose this case as a Posttraumatic Stress Disorder (309.81)? The reason is that there is no evidence of the presence of five of the six criteria listed in DSM-IV (p. 424). The only obvious criterion is D, sleep problems and difficulty concentrating, which is a symptom of many other conditions.

The reason for listing Dependent Personality Disorder on Axis II is that the dependency manifestations before the traumatic event had now become functional impairments for Michael. He was definitely not functioning with the ease he used to function, and he was doing things that he knew were not acceptable and of which he was ashamed, like making his little son stay with him in bed at night and calling his own father every day.

Case #3: Ann

Diagnosis: Axis I: Adjustment Disorder with mixed Anxiety and Depressed Mood (309.28).
Axis II: Obsessive-Compulsive Personality Disorder (301.4).

Rationale: From the information provided, the above diagnosis is appropriate for Ann. It must be stressed that no diagnosis should be carved in stone and that the door should always remain open for a modification, or even change, of the initial diagnosis.

The Axis I diagnosis is explained by her past suicidal thoughts, her anxiety about her perfect recovery, and her questions about the physical therapist's competence and possible attraction to her (or is it her projection?), as well as the questions about her new admirer.

The reason to use the above diagnosis on Axis II comes from her perfectionistic behavior corresponding to the symptomatology of the Obsessive-Compulsive Personality Disorder: her preoccupation with doing her physical therapy assignments perfectly, her moralistic judgment of self and others, her abandoning friends due to her intense devotion to her obligation to get completely well again, her rigidity and stubbornness–four of the criteria DSM-IV (p. 669) requires for this diagnosis.

Case #4: Max

Diagnosis: Axis I: Adjustment Disorder Unspecified (309.9).
Axis II: Avoidant Personality Disorder (301.82).

Rationale: Unspecified Adjustment Disorder is used because Max is obviously reacting in a maladaptive way without changing his socially withdrawn lifestyle, not taking effective steps to find another position or to finish his book. This subtype was chosen because his reaction to the psychosocial stressor of being fired is not classifiable in any of the other DSM-IV subtypes for this condition.

Regarding Axis II, there are enough indications to believe that this category describes his maladaptive behavior. Of the criteria listed by DSM-IV (p. 662) under Avoidant Personality Disorder, the following four apply to Max: (1) avoidance of occupational activities involving significant interpersonal contact, fearing criticism, disapproval and rejection; (2) unwillingness to be involved with people unless certain of being liked; (3) which is number 4 in DSM-IV, preoccupation with being criticized or rejected, as the long delay in finishing his book shows; (4) which is number 7 in DSM-IV, reluctance to engage in new activities for fear of embarrassment.

Because of all this factual evidence, we proceed with the diagnosis indicated above as *a working diagnosis*, until new evidence forces us to modify it.

SUMMARY

Since diagnosis is the fundamental step in any type of treatment, your attention to the area of Personality Disorders will be well worthwhile. Just because there is functional impairment after a stressful psychosocial event does not mean that the person can be diagnosed as suffering from Adjustment Disorder. As outlined in this chapter, a latent Personality Disorder is often elicited and made evident by a specific stressor or by an unusually stressful situation. The smart clinician will always look for the possibility of a Personality Disorder, not with a biased conviction that it must be there, but with a sense of professional responsibility that requires doing a thorough job.

6

General Treatment Principles

Only after the nature of Adjustment Disorder is clearly grasped can the clinician start to formulate a treatment plan. In general terms, it can be said that Adjustment Disorder follows a rather uniform pattern. There is a *psychosocial event* whose nature is of unusual severity from the individual's *perceptual system.* Because of this, the patient *overreacts emotionally*, often unleashing negative feelings about self, others, and life in general. Because of this emotional overreaction, the patient starts to engage in nonproductive, even *self-defeating, behavior.* After a while, this inappropriate behavior becomes a habit, which reinforces the negative feelings and the self-defeating action, thus creating *a vicious cycle* from which it becomes more difficult to break away as time goes by. To summarize, the Adjustment Disorder process follows five steps:

1. Psychosocially stressful event.
2. Negative perception.
3. Overreaction with negative feelings.
4. Inappropriate action.
5. Emotional vicious cycle.

As mentioned earlier, the psychosocial event is most often not necessarily stressful and disabling in itself. What makes it so is the individual's perception of it and the emotional significance that it carries for a particular person. Because of the way the event is perceived by the individual, it can become gravely stressful. In that case, there is always an emotional overreaction that disturbs the balance of the person's life. This overreaction has many components and levels of intensity, but it always includes negative self-talk, fostering of self-defeating imagery, and an increased sense of hopelessness, all contributing to the real experience of lack of emotional balance. Because of this disturbance, the person engages in inappropriate action, trying either to get rid of the negative feelings or to change the event, which frequently is not within the person's control. These inappropriate actions aggravate the negative emotions and strengthen the sense of helplessness and despair.

Because of the process of Adjustment Disorder, it is easy to see that its treatment must concern itself with the issue of the patient's perception of the stressful event that has created a state of anxiety and despair that reinforces itself in what we have described as a vicious cycle. By the time the person seeks psychotherapy, s/he is usually in a real state of despondency and hopelessness, with a very gloomy outlook for the future.

The clinician must be clear as to the treatment method to be used. We consider that the treatment modality (e.g., individual vs. group) and the treatment provider (e.g., psychiatrist, social worker, or mental health counselor) are less important than the treatment theory (e.g., psychodynamic, behavioral, medication, etc.). Because of this, we suggest the following four theoretical orientations, which we shall discuss presently:

1. Cognitive/Behavioral
2. Brief therapy
3. Group treatment
4. Tasks prescriptions

Regarding the *Cognitive/Behavioral* approach, we borrow from Ellis (1962) in the first place and from other important exponents of it (See Meichenbaum, 1977; Caballo, 1988, 1991; Beck & Freeman, 1990; Mahoney, 1992). Ellis' famous A-B-C model is helpful for the Adjustment Disorder patient. Briefly, we outline here what will become more comprehensible in the next chapter in which we summarize in detail eight ideal sessions with an Adjustment Disorder patient. The case of Mr. D., described in Chapter 2, followed these steps.

The clinician starts by inviting the patient to realize that s/he interprets what has happened or what is happening (the psychosocial stressor) in one way out of several possible interpretations and encourages him/her to try another interpretation. The patient is assisted to realize that the unhelpful interpretation s/he has chosen comes from beliefs, expectations, fears, past conditioning, and so on, and that it is now possible to try a different way of processing what is happening in the present. Our emphasis throughout, as will be perceived in the next chapter, is on aiding the patient to have an *inner experience* of the new reaction to the psychosocial stressor, what we describe with the Spanish word *vivencia.* It's not therapeutic just to talk about it. What produces change is to have a *vivencia* of the new way to perceive the painful situation and to react to it.

The *Brief Therapy* model provides us with useful tools to deal with Adjustment Disorders. The thinking of many authors has influenced our clinical approach (See Gilligan, 1990; Gordon, 1990; Gustafson, 1990; Haley, 1990; Polster, 1990). The main point in Brief Therapy is that "something (must) be done to achieve some end," as Haley put it. In other words, the goal of therapy is paramount from the very first minutes of the first session with a patient. In long-term therapy goals slowly emerge as weeks and months go by.

Because goals are concrete in Brief Therapy, as soon as positive improvement takes place, sessions can be spaced more widely apart while the patient strives after other goals. The focus is on how to change what is limiting the patient, not on what is wrong with him/her. The theory of resistance of long-term therapy places the whole treatment and termination in the hands of the therapist. In Brief Therapy the patient decides when s/he has improved sufficiently to end the therapeutic relationship because therapy is viewed as a means to *change,* not as a consolation and friendship, which is what long-term therapy may end up being for the patient in many cases. After several years of therapy, the original problem is still not resolved and more therapy is recommended as a solution. In Brief Therapy the patient's request for help to change specific aspects of his/her life is taken seriously; when the change occurs, the therapy ends. However, contrary to what long-term therapy believes, after the change the patient usually understands–has insight into–why s/he had the symptom that brought her/him into therapy.

We are justifying Brief Therapy for Adjustment Disorders rather than trying to make a case against long-term therapy or for Brief Therapy in general. Therefore, instead of interpretations, we use directives or prescriptions; instead of encouraging people to talk, we want them to work at changing; instead of focusing on the problem, we become obsessed with its solution or different ways of solving it from which the patient must choose the one that is best for him/her. Instead of accepting rationalizations about "not being ready to change," we use strategies to make the individual want to change now and to take responsibility for his/her own change with our assistance.

We are biased in favor of Group *theory*, for after patients have experienced the *vivencias* that change their outlook and attitude and after the constructive actions they have taken to improve their condition, the group provides support, correction through feedback, constructive criticism, a point of reference, and a forum for consultation. Patients who have not resolved the Adjustment Disorder in eight sessions have acquired all the tools they need to change, but are not using them. Rather than have them continue with private sessions, it is more effective for them to participate in a therapy group.

The final theoretical construct used beneficially with Adjustment Disorder patients refers to the *prescription of tasks* to be performed in between the therapy sessions. Strategic therapists, more so than other brief therapy practitioners, make these tasks a central part of their treatment. The tasks must be *individualized and agreed upon* with the patient's input. They must be *concrete, clear, and as simple as possible* in most cases. They also should be such that they *make the patient feel good* about performing them or about the results of the tasks.

Thus, a patient who finds it difficult to adapt to a new town to which the family has recently moved is instructed to make a list of things that are not so bad about the town and to concentrate on–visualize–a few of them every day. However, the patient is further instructed to see herself in one of the pleasant places of the new town doing something she enjoys and to practice this mind exercise again and again until it becomes easy for her to "visit" this place in her mind any time she needs to.

This task, as can be readily seen, fulfills the three main conditions or requirements mentioned above. It is tailored for this individual patient by its focus on the new place to which she has just moved. It is concrete and simple once she understands the prescription by practicing it with the clinician in the office before she starts doing it at home by herself alone. It is, finally, conducive to making her feel better.

Regarding this last requirement, it should be emphasized that the ultimate goal of therapy is to help the person *be* better. However, *feeling* better becomes an incentive to continue working on what is limiting the person's enjoyment of life and, thus, it is in most cases a useful therapeutic tool. Anything constructive that helps the patient feel better is therapeutic. In the example mentioned above, by practicing the prescribed task, the woman is learning to control her thoughts and, consequently, feels more empowered and freer. This feeling, on its own, tends to generalize and the person starts thinking of other areas of her life that she can bring under her control also.

Out of these four theoretical orientations, and keeping in mind the five progressive steps in the development of Adjustment Disorder, we can draw some general treatment principles for patients with this diagnosis.

The first principle of treatment focuses on the patient's perception: *All stressful psychosocial events need to be reframed or redefined.* Then the Second Principle, below, qualifies this: *To feel right, have the right thoughts.* All kinds of expressions of helplessness are heard from these patients because all look at the event only as devastating. Therefore, clinicians are insistent in the reframing process: "If three years from now you realized that something good came out of this situation," "If you had to advise someone in the same situation whom you care about," "The way you will see all this in twenty years," etc., are the new thoughts the patient needs in order to feel and act differently.

But because perception is not just an intellectual phenomenon but involves also imagination, in reframing, too, imagination must be involved. Patients are taught to activate their imagination as much as they activate it when they worry. Now, however, the images and mental pictures that patients will allow are going to be pictures of empowerment, self-enhancement, and hope. If the patient mentioned in the earlier example finds herself sad and unhappy every time she thinks of the friends she left behind, she is taught to think of the "less than bad" things that are real in the new place, as we indicated in this chapter in the case of task prescriptions.

The second principle of feeling right through having the right thoughts is based on Rational Emotive Therapy. The patient is assisted in realizing that every feeling is preceded by a thought and that it is easier to control feelings if one watches over one's thoughts. With practice, this will soon avoid the overreaction to a stressful event and help the person cope better with it. In Chapter 8 on self-therapy, many easy techniques for patients to practice will be proposed. The value of this principle is that it provides the patient with a new sense of mastery over the symptoms. After that, they often wonder about the causes of the overreaction and the Adjustment Disorder and may, then, enter into an analytical introspection in order to obtain an answer to that question. But Principle Two allows them to get to the point where they are interested in getting to the root of the problem.

The third principle, *Constructive action is worth the effort*, emphasizes the patient's responsibility and the need to accept "effort." It's not going to be easy but it's doable. There will be pain, but it is short-term pain for long-term gain, as the saying goes. The therapist invites the patient to remember other situations in his/her life where effort, pain, and sacrifice brought about positive results. With this "evidence" from the patient's own history, the new task is to determine which actions out of many possibilities should be taken up first.

Responsibility, active involvement in taking constructive steps to change, modification of unreasonable expectations (from "Things have to change," "So and So must come to my rescue and solve my problem," etc., to "I have to change," "I have to help myself," etc.), all enter into the Third Principle and the clinician's task is to facilitate the taking of constructive action by the patient. This "action" does not necessarily have to be a drastic change. In many cases it can be compared to baby steps. As long as they are taken in the right direction, they are the constructive action that is needed.

Thus, Principle Three serves as a tool to check the validity of the diagnosis. In genuine cases of Adjustment Disorder, patients welcome this assistance to engage in constructive action. On the other hand, if they do not take constructive action, chances are great that there was a misdiagnosis to begin with. The right diagnosis has to be established, such as a form of depression or a Personality Disorder, and the appropriate treatment for that condition must be initiated. It is obvious that to use treatment for Adjustment Disorders will not be effective for these other cases.

These three are the basic principles underlying any therapeutic intervention for Adjustment Disorders. As is evident, following the already cited Ellis (1962) model, they refer, first, to patients' perception of the awful situation they have gone through or their "thinking" about it. Secondly, the three treatment principles for Adjustment Disorders relate to patients' emotional reaction to their own perception of the event or their "feelings" affected by the perception of the event. Finally, they focus on the behaviors they have undertaken in reaction to the stressor, but which only aggravate the general situation, or on the "actions" that must be changed in order to recover from the traumatic event that initiated the symptoms the patients are complaining of in therapy.

It is useful for the mental health practitioner to check frequently in order to monitor the therapeutic procedure. Nothing in the clinical work can contradict these principles, which are the skeleton of what the Adjustment Disorder patient needs in order to recover.

For instance, as we shall see in the next chapter, in the first session, the goals of treatment are discussed. If the clinician is not careful, the overall goal of recovery might seem overwhelming to patients and thus undermine them. In line with the principles mentioned above, the clinician will determine with the patients what concrete and simple action they can take during the following week or 10 days in order to start countering the nonproductive behaviors that they have engaged in as a reaction to the psychosocial stressor.

With all of the above in view, the clinician can now proceed to treat Adjustment Disorder according to the managed care model. This method includes the following seven elements:

1. Diagnosis.
2. Immediate intervention.
3. Homework or task prescriptions.
4. Environmental changes.
5. Building support networks.
6. Overcoming obstacles and resistance.
7. Therapist availability.

Since all therapy, medical or psychological, is a maneuver designed to produce some change or improvement, the question of goals is one of the first to be considered. It is realistic to distinguish between immediate, intermediate, and ultimate goals. In the managed care treatment for Adjustment Disorders, the *immediate goal* is to help patients start experiencing relief right away and after the first session of therapy. This means that the clinician takes a very active though equally respectful role, to be explained in the next chapter, in aiding patients to change their current perception of the situation.

As indicated above, unless Adjustment Disorder patients start to feel good very early in treatment, they are in danger of discontinuing therapy. The clinician views the immediate goal as something to be accomplished in the first session. Feeling good may mean experiencing less anxiety, but it also may mean that patients have accepted a slightly different manner of considering the stressful event, themselves, and their world; consequently, they have discovered some new way of reacting to the whole situation.

Thus, the immediate goal includes also the vital task of motivating patients to continue in treatment and to do their part by following the prescribed tasks. It is obvious that if the clinician does not obtain the serious commitment of the patient to work together in order to cure and resolve the symptoms producing the patient's functional impairment, nothing beneficial can happen. Therefore, the immediate goal is twofold: Help the patient feel more hopeful or less distressed and engage him/her in treatment.

Regarding the *intermediate goal*, this is an intense process during which patients learn effective ways, both mental and behavioral, of reacting to the stressful event, as opposed to the ineffective manner in which they have handled the identifiable psychosocial stressor to date. Emphasis must be placed on learning both mental and behavioral ways, with minimal stress and pain, to cope with the psychosocial occurrence that precipitated the symptoms and the current misery of functional impairment. Not only do patients learn mental techniques to change their manner of thinking, they practice them first in the consulting room with the help and under the direction of the clinician, and then they repeat the practice many times alone until the next session with the professional.

Similarly, with the behavioral tasks, the clinician literally teaches the patient what to do, how to do it, how frequently to do it, how to handle failures or mistakes in practicing the prescribed tasks, and how to record the progress made. Because of this "educational" role, the mental health practitioner requests a report on the patient's progress and discusses with the patient what consequences will ensue if the tasks are not done or are done poorly.

As mentioned in reference to the immediate goal, here, too, if the patient does not cooperate it will be impossible to reach the *ultimate goal*, which consists in the adoption by the patient of a new and different way of reacting to stressful situations and events in the future. Because of the rehearsing, role playing, and coaching that belong to the intermediate goal, the patient can be helped to truly adopt new ways of reacting to painful and difficult situations henceforward. For this, more of the same "educational" interventions just enumerated are used repeatedly.

The ultimate goal is the certitude of both the patient and the clinician that the old overreaction to "bad things" is not going to be the same that brought the patient to treatment. Without this ultimate goal, treatment is not finished, especially under the managed care model, because patients have not yet generalized what they have learned in the particular situation that motivated them to request therapy. It is like people who memorize a few sentences in a foreign language to be able to go on a brief business trip to that country. Even though they "speak" the language when they use the memorized phrases, they do not know the language because they cannot construct sentences of their own.

In the long run, treatment that zeroes in on one specific problem without having obtained the generalization of learning may solve the problem, but does not change what originated it. It is more cost-effective and more genuine for patients to learn to generalize from the current problem to other similar situations and, thus, to be able to handle them effectively thanks to the one problem that they have resolved successfully. The old proverb about the difference between giving someone a fish to assuage present hunger and teaching the same person how to fish so that s/he may never be hungry again comes to mind. The more technical distinction between first-order change and second-order change, made by Watzlawick, Weakland, and Fisch (1974), is precise and less colorful: "There are two different types of change: one that occurs within a given system which itself remains unchanged [first-order change] and one whose occurrence changes the system itself [second-order change]" (p. 10).

If psychotherapy is worth its name, it changes the system, namely, the individual, his interpretation of events, his attitude, fears, dreams, prejudices, self-imposed limitations, and so on. Because of this, we hold strongly to the position that the ultimate goal of therapy for Adjustment Disorders is second-order change. The clinician influences the patient to never again want to overreact in the ineffective and limiting way she did in the case at hand because she has learned how not to do it.

Now that the goals have been considered, it might be helpful to summarize the steps of the treatment proper (i.e., after the diagnosis has been formulated). They are basically seven, even though each comprises more than one part:

1. Define the problem of functional impairment.
   Affirm existence of problem.
   Connect symptoms/functional impairment to stressor.
2. With patient, set tentative goal for improvement.
3. Identify strengths and personal, mental, social, and other resources to overcome the negative effects of stressor shown in functional impairment.
4. Form a detailed, concrete, attainable plan of action to be started right away in order to attain step #2 above.
5. Foresee and try to overcome obstacles, both external (such

as family, social contacts, and real circumstances of living) and internal (resistance, lethargy, old bad habits, and false beliefs).

6. Practice between therapy sessions the learned behaviors, both mental and external, in different life situations and notice difficulties in order to prepare better for future circumstances in which the old, ineffective reactions may tend to return.
7. Monitor the progress made and/or the troubles encountered in the practice of the therapy plan in order to have a constant corrective mechanism. This is gained through introspection and behavioral monitoring until the patient realizes that he has changed the attitudes, expectations, fears, and reactions that were involved in his Adjustment Disorder.

Regarding these seven treatment steps, it should be remembered that they overlap considerably. For instance, the identification of strengths and personal resources of step #3 must happen all along, as a habitual concern necessary for a complete recovery. Again, the awareness of "obstacles" of any type and the monitoring of one's progress are also not to be limited to merely fixed points in the treatment process. Finally, even the diagnosis of Adjustment Disorder deserves constant attention because of DSM-IV's criteria, such as the one regarding the duration of the symptoms, as was mentioned in Chapter 4 on Diagnosis. It is also to be kept in mind due to the relationship of Adjustment Disorder with Bereavement (V62.82) and even with Posttraumatic Stress Disorder (309.81).

The principles of treatment discussed in this chapter assume always that the clinician takes an active role in each psychotherapy session. Mere listening is inappropriate when treating patients with Adjustment Disorder. Active reframing, guidance, suggestions, and teaching of specific mind exercises, as well as prescription of concrete behavioral tasks and much more, are useful and, consequently, acceptable.

Clinicians who come from traditional therapy schools, including the psychodynamic, will need to retrain themselves to feel comfortable with the more active techniques. Because of its theoretical simplicity and its commonsensical approach, with genuine respect for the client, the Ericksonian Brief Therapy approach (see Zeig & Gilligan, 1990, and Zeig, 1994) is especially welcome for its power to unlock potentials of the individual.

The following chapter assumes that the clinician has already become comfortable with the methods of brief therapy, specifically as exemplified in the teachings of Milton H. Erickson.

7

Psychotherapy for Adjustment Disorders

Out of the seven steps outlined at the end of the previous chapter comes the *Summary Outline of AD Treatment* presented here. Later comes the *Detailed Session-by-Session Outline*, a more specific explanation of psychotherapeutic strategies for AD. The following *Summary Outline* for treatment may be used as a quick reference by the busy clinician. It may help as a guide to recognizing where the patient is in treatment and what should be the next step to take.

SUMMARY OUTLINE OF AD TREATMENT

First Session

Objectives

- Define problem: symptoms, impairment of patient.
- Formulate or confirm diagnosis.
- Develop therapeutic relationship and availability.
- Establish goals (solutions).
- Teach and practice cognitive restructuring.
- Prescribe a specific practice as home task.

Strategies

- Help patient define presenting problem concretely.
- Establish accurate diagnosis.
- Carry out strategic questioning about functional impairment.
- Set therapeutic practice to:
    a) reframe problem and
    b) avoid problem-related feelings.

Prescription

- Perform daily repetition of practice learned and done in office.
- Keep written record of practice.
- Make appointment for following week.

Second Session

Objectives

- Confirm diagnosis.
- Review compliance with prescription.
- Reinforce practice of First Session.
- Encourage specific constructive behaviors.

Strategies

- Review progress as recorded by patient.
- Check patient's reactions to prescribed practice.
- Track behavior towards solution.
- Expand on mind exercise of First Session.

Prescription

- Continue home practice, including written record.
- Make appointment for one or two weeks depending on progress made by patient.

Third Session

Objectives

- Evaluate progress to date.
- Reinforce positive effort to improve.
- Reframe therapy as learning and growth experience.
- Encourage more solution-oriented concrete behaviors.

Strategies

- Discuss last prescription in detail.
- Review patient's ability to reframe stressor.
- Go over possible negative actions, places, people to avoid until next appointment.
- Practice mental rehearsal.

Prescription

- Prepare written statement on learning and growth experience.
- If progress is positive, make appointment for two weeks later. If no satisfactory progress, make appointment for next week.

Fourth Session

Objectives

- Solidify gains.
- Prepare patient for possible setbacks.
- Prepare patient for continuing own work without therapy.

Strategies

- Review compliance with prescriptions.
- Analyze possible setbacks.
- Provide strategies to avoid setback.
- Teach technique to reinforce positive feelings.

Prescription

- Contact "positive people" in patient's life.
- Continue practice of mind exercises.
- Make appointment for at least two weeks.

Fifth Session

Objectives

- Reinforce gains from previous sessions.
- Practice mental rehearsal of fulfilled life without therapy.
- Evaluate and commit to continue practices by self.
- Introduce idea of support group if needed in future.

Strategies

- Review prescriptions from previous sessions.
- Review setbacks, if any, and repeat practices learned since starting psychotherapy.
- Explain availability and advantage of support group if needed in future.
- Practice visualization projecting "new" life–with family, at work, with friends, others.

Prescription

- Practice visualization once a day.
- Keep written record of above.
- Set appointment for two or three weeks later.

Sixth Session

Objectives

- Reinforce patient's ability to be own "therapist" re: AD.
- Review practice of visualization since previous session.

- Apply "learning experiences" from therapy to other areas of patient's life; be concrete.

Strategies

- Teach and encourage practice of "Do-it-yourself-therapy."
- Focus on positive gains and benefits to patient from them.
- Discuss "mechanisms" of adjustment learned so far in order to generalize gains made.
- Visualize himself/herself in a support group.

Prescription

- Practice mind and behavioral exercises to rehearse new attitudes and beliefs in diverse areas of patient's life.
- Set appointment for at least three weeks later.
- Request one phone call in 10 to 12 days.

Seventh Session

Objectives

- Follow up on previous session.
- Provide new mental technique to facilitate adjustment to new, similar situations.
- Acknowledge and "own" progress made so far in order to strengthen hope for future.
- Check patient's reaction to possibility of support group after individual therapy is terminated.

Strategies

- Discuss setbacks, if any; analyze patient's ways of handling them with strategies learned in therapy.
- Ask about possibility of support group.
- Teach and practice BRIMS (Breathing, Relaxation, Imagery, Messages, Sign) as new mind technique to abort psychological problems due to adjustment situations in

the future (second and third objectives above).
- Give patient audiotape of BRIMS.

Prescription

- Practice BRIMS at least every other day and make written record of practice.
- Set appointment for at least three weeks later.

Eighth Session

Objectives

- Review and solidify gains made in psychotherapy.
- Termination of psychotherapy.

Strategies

- Review adjustment to original stressor and other aspects of patient's life.
- Review practice of BRIMS and repeat practice if needed.
- Arrange for possible telephone contact after therapy is finished; discuss fee for this service.
- Refer to support group if advisable.
- Confirm termination within framework of gains made.

DETAILED SESSION-BY-SESSION OUTLINE FOR TREATMENT OF AD

First Session

Objectives

1. Formulate diagnosis, at least tentatively.
2. Begin the building of trust and rapport: "Your problem is not unique. There is an effective cure. Treatment involves

your cooperation. I am here to help you resolve your problem and go back to living your life fully."

3. Address the Adjustment Disorder problem, i.e., patient's impairment, giving the patient a valid sense of looking forward to a solution: thoughts to foster and actions to take and avoid, so that patient can start "moving" towards a solution right away.

Strategies

1. Help patient clarify and define the impairment caused by the Adjustment Disorder: "What happens to you when you think of (the psychosocial stressor)? How does your body react? In what part of your body do you feel its impact?"
2. Establish diagnosis (See Chapter 4).
3. Ask, "What do you say to yourself about this problem?" In patient's answer, remark any negative, self-defeating statements, such as, "I shouldn't feel this way. I'm acting like a baby," etc.
4. Inquire also, "What mental images come to mind when you say to yourself (such and such)?" In patient's reply, identify any negative elements.
5. Report to patient your awareness of the negative elements in his/her answers to the above two questions and ask, "How can you change what you say to yourself, avoiding the negative elements and still staying within the truth?" Help patient if s/he has difficulty coming up with less negative statements and mental images. Once an acceptable statement is found and agreed upon, invite patient to repeat it, first out loud and then silently to himself/herself in a quiet, relaxed way.
6. Then ask, "How were you feeling when you said that (repetition of the positive statement of [5.] above) to yourself?" If answer is too general (e.g., "Pretty good"), ask her/him to repeat the "new" statement a few times while self-monitoring how the body is reacting to it. You watch also for the slightest indication of tension in the patient's demeanor,

breathing, or expression. Do this until patient reports a better sense than before.

7. Then analyze with patient the "things" that came to mind when he/she is repeating the new (more positive) statement. And from these "things," point out any images, memories, feelings, bodily sensations that might be both constructive and beneficial to the patient.
8. Practice again with the patient embellishing the positive images that you detected in (7.) above, in connection with the new self-suggestions of (6.) above. You may audiotape this practice so that the patient is able to repeat it to himself/herself, as per your prescription below.

   Example: If patient said in (3.) above, "I can't take this any longer," and visualized in (4.) her becoming sleepless and sick to her stomach, the therapist may suggest an alternative statement to use, e.g., "I have gone through many difficult things in the past and I have survived!" Then, the therapist may suggest a peaceful image to go with that statement, e.g., mountains, seashore, a quiet room in a museum, etc. In this mental place, according to the patient's preference, the therapist invites the patient to see herself/himself repeating the triumphant refrain, "I have survived! I can survive this too!"

Prescription

Prescribe that patient practice the above (8.) every day and that s/he keep a *written* record of the practice. If this cannot be done one day, the practice should be made up the following day or on the weekend. Emphasize this as a necessary practice for rapid improvement.

Note: Since the first therapy session is crucial in establishing rapport, as most authors teach, make sure that you are able to give the patient your full attention, without any other worries or distractions in your mind. No telephone calls should be accepted, no interruptions allowed, no rearranging of papers from the previous patient. Objective 2, the building of trust, depends greatly on your positive firmness, your professionally friendly attitude, and your convinced assurance that Adjustment Disorder is not an indication of mental illness or "craziness," but a frequent overreaction, painful and disturbing, to be sure, of the human organism (body, mind, and spirit) in an effort to adapt to a new situation. As Epstein (1994) explains, using his global model of personality theory, the *Cognitive Experiential Self-Theory* or CEST, the organism tries to integrate all experiences. When it cannot do so because they are too painful, it becomes impaired and shows behavioral symptoms.

In many cases it is useful to explain Adjustment Disorders in Rational Emotive Therapy (RET) terms: It's not what happens to us but the way we react to a difficult situation that produces the problem. The solution lies in changing our perception and our reaction. Therapy teaches us to modify our perception through reframing and to react differently to the same situation through cognitive and behavioral means.

RET is also useful for making the patient aware of the importance of his/her own thoughts. The sequence of *Think-Feel-Act* is explained in reverse order: actions come from the way you feel and the way you feel is the result of your thoughts.

These easy-to-understand principles lay the foundation for the work that is to come in the following therapy sessions .

A final word of caution for this first session is for you to be relaxed and in no hurry, especially when you guide your patient through the mind exercise described under Strategies (3.) to (8.).

Second Session

Objectives

1. Confirm or modify diagnosis.
2. Help patient realize importance of own thinking in the way s/he feels, based on the last session's prescription.
3. Encourage patient to increase the activities that contribute to the diminution of his/her impairment by starting to effect some environmental changes.

Strategies

1. Check on patient's compliance with the prescription given in the first session.
   (a) If patient complied at least every other day proceed to (2.) below.
   (b) If patient did not comply, state something like this: "Last time you were here, when we first met, you practiced with me the mind exercise regarding your negative thoughts and how to change them for your benefit. I understood you felt that it could help you to learn to do it on your own. Remember? You agreed to repeat this practice at home. But things came up, and you didn't have a chance to practice it."
      - If patient has a good reason for the lack of compliance, renew your previous prescription, guide patient again through the same practice in the office as in first session, and proceed to the next step.
      - If patient has no good reason, review the diagnosis, according to Chapter 4. If the early Adjustment Disorder diagnosis need not be changed, go to the next step.
      - Didactically explain that Adjustment Disorder is a function of *one's inner reaction* to a psychosocial stressor, applying this generic concept to the patient's current condition; that one's reaction can be changed and improved by one's learning how to do so in therapy; that there is no pill or magic to do this. One has to do it oneself. And the practice learned in the first session is an effective method to produce this change.
      - Obtain patient's commitment to practice the prescription until next week.
      - Guide patient through the same practice, as in 1(b) above, and proceed to (2.) below.
2. Ask patient if s/he has noticed any change in symptoms. Be as specific as possible. Don't accept a general, "Things are better" answer. Ask for concrete examples.
   (a) If things are better, proceed to (3.) below.

(b) If the symptoms are the same or worse, find out *how* patient practiced the prescribed mind exercise.
- If practice was adequate–right frequency, without distractions, following the method taught last session–encourage continued practice and proceed to step (3.) below.

(c) If the patient's practice was *not* adequate, explain again how to do it and lead patient through the same mind exercise again, as in the first session.

3. Review patient's environment.

(a) Track patient's behavior in
- Daily schedule: workday, weekend, last vacation, etc.
- Interpersonal relations: work, home, family, friends.
- Interests and hobbies: past and current.
- General dietary habits.
- Physical activities.
- Any other aspects of patient's "world," such as religion, civic or political involvement, and the like.

(b) Rate 3(a) in terms of situations, activities, and persons that are pleasant, enjoyable, and positive, as well as those that are stressful, unpleasant, and difficult. Ask which of these make symptoms worse and which make them better. Introduce the concept of *nurturing* and *toxic* for patient to use to identify different persons, situations, and events in his/her life.

(c) Discuss *practical* means to engage patient more in nurturing behaviors and interactions and less in toxic ones until the next therapy session.

Prescription

1. Prescribe that patient practice daily 1(b) above and that s/he keep a written record of performance. Suggest a simple way of recording the mind practice, giving it a grade of A, B, or C, depending on how well it went each day.
2. Patient will keep a log to become aware of events, persons, and situations that are nurturing or toxic for her/him.

Third Session

Objectives

1. Evaluate progress made so far.
2. Reinforce patient's efforts to improve.
3. Reframe the whole therapy experience as a learning and growth opportunity.
4. Encourage continued "work" on the patient's part.

Strategies

1. Check the two written records kept by patient since last session:
   (a) If patient kept adequate records of his/her mind practice and of the toxic/nurturing events since last session, proceed to (2.) below.
   (b) If patient did *not* keep an adequate record of her/his practice, proceed in a manner similar to 1(b) in the second session.
2. Ask patient about progress made, i.e., less impairment, which means more empowerment, and insist on minute details of what patient reports as "progress." Reinforce any small progress and encourage continuation of patient's efforts.
3. Ask patient what "lessons" s/he is learning from this whole Adjustment Disorder experience: the event that triggered the patient's impairment or symptoms, the initial reactions to the stressor, the decision to seek therapy, the patient's expectations of it, the beginning of the psychotherapy process, the progress made so far, both in behavior as well as in mental attitude, and the current feelings about the entire experience.

   Pay special attention to the patient's associations of the identifiable psychosocial stressor with other aspects of his/her life. Take always a positive attitude towards whatever progress was made so far. This conveys the message to the patient that, in spite of other difficult situations in the past, the patient is moving forward and is not using them as excuses in the current case.

Prescription

For the next therapy session, patient

1. Writes an introspective statement about Strategy 3.
2. Continues the daily practice of the mind exercise and keeps a written record of it, as before.
3. If progress was real, make next appointment for two weeks later. If you are not satisfied with the progress made, give patient an appointment for the following week.

Note: The third session is especially important because by now the patient must be thoroughly committed to therapy. At this point the prognosis can be determined. The prognosis is negative when the patient has given lip service to the psychotherapy process, but has not really changed behavior or attitude. Discuss this with the patient in terms of possible secondary gains from the impairment/symptoms. This is the point at which you ascertain whether there are enough indications for a diagnosis of Personality Disorder (see Chapter 5).

Three possibilities present themselves. Change the diagnosis in Axis II and obtain permission from the managed care company to continue psychotherapy under the new diagnosis. The second choice is to bring home to the patient the importance of "working" in order to improve his/her symptoms triggered by the identifiable psychosocial stressor. Third, to dismiss the patient if the previous two options are not possible, because treatment cannot be continued without her/his serious and active cooperation, which, in turn, is not possible without the patient's commitment to improve.

If the patient insists on the second option, above, to continue treatment, you must firmly assert that the following week will be a test: If s/he does not do his/her part, therapy cannot continue.

The question is: How will you know that the patient is telling you the truth? Next week s/he shows you an impeccable written record of practice in the two areas of the mind exercise and of the toxic/

nurturing situations. S/he further tells you how much all this is helping. But the whole tale is a lie. You should keep in mind the possibility of Malingering (DSM-IV, V65.2) if your questions lead you to that suspicion or even to that diagnosis.

Fourth Session

Objectives

1. In the case of a patient who falls under the circumstances of the Note at the end of the previous session, make sure that s/he has committed him/herself to the work of therapy, as indicated there.
2. Solidify the gains made so far.
3. Prepare patient for possible setbacks.
4. Prepare patient for continuing his/her "own" therapy without obtaining psychotherapy by a provider.

Strategies

1. Review compliance with prescriptions given at the end of last session.
   (a) If patient wrote statement about what this experience taught her/him and how it has, indeed, been a growth experience, go to Strategy 3 on page 91.
   (b) If patient did not write the prescribed statement, inquire the reasons for not doing it.
      - If reasons are acceptable, request that it be mailed to you before the next session so that you have the statement when you see him/her again.
      - If reasons are not acceptable, go to 1(d).
   (c) Ask about patient's keeping written records (from last session's Prescriptions).
      - If patient kept the written records as prescribed, go to 2. on the following page.
      - If patient did not fulfill the prescriptions from your last session, go to the next step.

(d) Assuming a secondary gain from the patient's lack of compliance, explain that therapy will be discontinued at the next session if patient does not cooperate; that psychotherapy, more so than medical therapy, necessitates the patient's taking full responsibility for progress.

(e) Ask if patient wants to work *now*, in the rest of the session.
- If the answer is Yes, repeat what was done in the third session, Strategies section.
- If the answer is No, dismiss the patient until the next session, one week from this date, repeating the prescriptions of the last session.

2. Address yourself to the issue of possible setbacks, not to look forward to them but not to be surprised if they happen. Patient should consider them as detours or parentheses in the process of therapy and cure. Despite the setbacks, the patient's task is to get back on the right track as soon as possible by returning to what has been learned in therapy so far.

(a) Mentally rehearse with the patient a situation where s/he resumes the symptoms that brought him/her to therapy. What would the patient say to herself/himself? What would s/he do and not do? What toxic situations and persons would s/he avoid and which nurturing ones would s/he seek out and foster? Emphasize the advantage of keeping the practices learned so far as a preventive measure.

3. Establish a network of nurturing/positive people. Help patient think of five or six of those people whom s/he can contact without difficulty. As long as you help the patient to come up with one nurturing person, you can proceed.
4. Rehearse with the patient how s/he would contact that positive/nurturing person: by phone, by sending a greeting card, or by meeting in some way.

Prescription

1. Patient should continue with previous Prescription 2. as a preventive measure in order to avoid possible setbacks and as a strengthening measure in case they happen.

2. Patient should make a *solid* list of at least three nurturing/ positive people.
3. Patient should make an effective attempt, by phone, mail, or in person, to contact his/her positive/nurturing people in order to remind them that they are important to her/ him. (Go over this with patient.)
4. Make next appointment for double the interval that existed between sessions so far. In other words, if you saw patient on an average of once a week, make the next appointment for two weeks from today's date.

Note: Without being too rigid about it, you should consider that the fourth session is, in many cases, the middle point of therapy for Adjustment Disorders. For this reason, it is helpful to tell the patient explicitly during this session that you believe s/he is ready to do what you prescribe. However, if you do not believe in the patient's readiness, don't say it; reconsider the diagnosis once more, especially in reference to Axis II in DSM-IV.

If you believe that the patient is making good progress within the Adjustment Disorder diagnosis, this is the time to remind him/her that you are available for a very brief consultation over the telephone *if there is a real need* on the patient's part. This will help you assess the patient's regained strength at this point in therapy. If s/he does not call, the indications of strength are better than if s/he starts leaving messages for you in your answering service. A word of advice: Don't rush to answer the patient's call. Waiting a few hours or until the following day fulfills two objectives: It conveys the message that you trust the patient to handle whatever came up, and it avoids reinforcing the telephone contact that you introduced "in case of a real need."

Fifth Session

Objectives

1. Reinforcement of previous session's gains regarding means used by patient in order to experience her/himself stronger and able to handle future difficulties.

2. Active mental rehearsal of a fulfilled life without the help of a therapist. This practice is taught in order for the patient to start his/her own "therapy."
3. A firm commitment to become his/her "own therapist." Once the commitment is obtained, plans will be made to establish and keep daily "sessions" (See Prescriptions below).

Strategies

1. Obtain a detailed report on patient's practice of the prescriptions given last time: (i.) visualization, (ii.) written record, (iii.) contact "positive people."
   (a) If done, continue on to 2. below.
   (b) If not done, inquire into causes for lack of compliance.
   - If reasons are acceptable, go to (2.) on page 94.
   - If reasons are not acceptable, ask patient to reverse roles with you: What would s/he think, say, do if the therapist were the patient and s/he were the therapist?

   Discuss the patient's response and reasoning and obtain commitment to continue. If you do not sense that the commitment is genuine, terminate therapy and dismiss the patient with the argument that s/he is not ready at this point to make the necessary effort to improve and resolve the problem of Adjustment Disorder that brought her/him to therapy. Add that you will be available if in the future s/he truly wants to change.

   This way of dismissing the patient, without any coloration of personal annoyance on your part, often produces good results. The patient may ask right away to continue treatment with you or may call you over the phone to ask for another chance. In the latter case, be brief over the phone. Ask why you should believe her/him now and, if you are satisfied, make a new appointment. When you resume treatment after this "crisis," always ask the patient what reassurances you will have about his/her new resolve and do not continue treatment until you are satisfied that the patient is now serious about treatment.

On the other hand, if after the role reversal you sense that the patient's commitment is real, proceed to the next step.

2. Review the issue of setbacks from last session and repeat the mental rehearsal of the previous session, under 2(a).
3. Review the patient's list of "positive people" in his/her life. Has patient thought of new people to add to her/his network?
4. Has patient contacted some of these "positive people" in her/his life?, How did it go?, etc.
5. Ask patient to visualize a fulfilled life without the help of therapy. You may suggest something like this: "Put yourself in the near future when you have already resolved all the problems you had because of (mention the psychosocial stressor responsible for the Adjustment Disorder). Take your time and let me know when you are there in your mind, in your imagination."

   When patient lets you know by a grunt, a word, a facial expression or other movement, you continue. If there is no response, be calm and tell the patient to take his/her time, to let any images come smoothly to her/his mind, to make believe that s/he is already cured, happy, free from all the limitations, impairment, and symptoms. And again, ask something like, "Is it in your mind?" or "Are you OK?" or "Are you there?" Then continue.

   "Notice how wonderful you feel. You've been through a lot and now you are free. You feel proud of yourself, of your great accomplishment. After all that, you deserve to feel great. Stay with that good feeling and feel terrific for a little while. No rush. Now, go slowly over a regular day: what you do–take your time–the people you deal with, the places where you are, your meals, and everything else that you do in a regular day. Notice how good you feel. Enjoy that positive feeling again. Take your time to be soaked by that good sense. Notice that nothing takes away your inner sense of peace and well-being." Continue this as needed, emphasizing every gain made and all the positive feelings about the patient's recovery.

If time permits, do the same focusing on work, or on the patient's family, or on when the patient is alone, or on special occasions, like holidays, and so on. In any event, go slowly, encourage the patient to really concentrate on the scenes that you suggest (for which the closing of the eyes is very conducive), and invite constantly the engagement of as many senses as are involved in each scene. Remember that even though in our language we refer to the mind's eye, the mind can also replicate the sensations of all the other senses. If the patient wants to talk during this practice and to let you know what is going through his/her mind, gently discourage it and assure her/him that you'll talk about it in a little while, following the practice.

After a few minutes of this mind exercise, discuss with the patient in detail what went on in her/his mind when you were guiding her/him through that visualization. In this discussion, pay special attention to any constructive, positive elements in what the patient reports. Encourage the patient to linger during the day on the situations that the patient envisions as being fulfilling, enjoyable, and rewarding.

If you feel comfortable doing it, you will help the patient more effectively if you use an audiotape machine to record what you are saying so that the patient will be able to fulfill the following prescription.

Very Important! Reframe this practice as "Self-Therapy" and move on to the Prescriptions.

Prescription

1. To practice daily the above mind exercise by repeating what the patient did in your office. If you audiotaped the visualization, stress that the patient must "get into" the tape, not just listen to it as if it were a taped lecture. For this, s/he needs a few minutes of solitude and privacy without interruptions of any kind.

   Request that the patient keep a written record of this practice, scoring it with an "A" for *very good*, "B" for *good*, "C" for *not good*, and "O" for *not done that day.*

2. Again, make an appointment for at least two weeks from the date of this fifth session.

Sixth Session

Objectives

1. To strengthen the patient's readiness to continue his/her own therapy, without the help of a therapist, based on the patient's positive experience with visualization, as taught in the last therapy session.
2. Review of all the gains made during psychotherapy thus far.
3. Application of what was learned from therapy to other areas of the patient's life that may benefit from a better adjustment to them.

Strategies

1. Inquire about the practice of "self-therapy" and go over the written record of the practice with the "grades" that the patient gave himself/herself. Answer any questions and then go over the same practice once more with the patient, but spending less time than during the previous session. After this abbreviated practice, discuss with the patient how it went, how it was different from other times, how s/he can do it even better, etc.
2. Ask patient to tell you how things have improved in her/his life in the last eight or nine weeks. Give patient credit for what s/he has done by following the prescriptions of therapy. Encourage patient to feel good about the improvements and to be proud of the accomplishments.
3. Because the patient has discovered new ways of adjusting to the psychosocial stressor that triggered the symptoms, you should now discuss the "mechanisms" of adjustment that have produced the current good results. These mechanisms are mostly internal, like thoughts, beliefs, and atti-

tudes, but also behaviors, things, places, or persons to either avoid or to frequent.

Then discuss how to use the same mental mechanisms in other areas of his/her life that could benefit from better adjustment. Give the patient enough time to become aware of the psychological process of generalization that can become useful–that from the experience of therapy for a specific problem, s/he can apply or generalize what was learned to many other areas in life.

Prescriptions

1. Patient will have a relaxed conversation with one of his/her "positive persons" on 3. above.
2. Patient will continue to practice visualization as in previous weeks and keep a written record of the same.
3. Make a new appointment for at least three weeks from this session.

Note: Under normal circumstances, the managed care company will grant two more sessions to a person with an Adjustment Disorder diagnosis. Because of this, you must be sure that the patient is fully involved in his/her recovery. One area that needs the therapist's attention is that of visualization. Make sure that the patient is doing it correctly, giving it 20 to 30 concentrated minutes each time, without interruptions of any kind, having understood the process, rather than following a rigid script; being satisfied with a relaxed concentration rather than aiming at some vivid, hallucination-like mental picture. Often, people who claim they cannot visualize, have unrealistic expectations and need to be told that if they can describe in great detail their living room, with colors, sizes, distances, and proportions, they *can* visualize because what they just did in describing their living room *is* visualization.

The other area of concern for the clinician is the behavioral one. Make sure that the patient does have a small list of positive people and that s/he contacts them and has started a relationship with them.

Finally, you have to make sure that a process of psychological vaccination has taken place regarding possible relapses and that *generalization* has taken place. In order to obtain this assurance, you will find it helpful to ask the person to place himself/herself mentally in tough situations that would normally elicit extraordinary stress, anxiety, or fear and apprehension. This will serve as desensitization for the patient.

Seventh Session

Objectives

1. Follow up on previous session in order to take care of any setbacks.
2. Provide patient with new mental technique to facilitate adjustment to new situations.
3. Reinforce patient's conviction about continuing to do well without formal therapy by applying what s/he has learned in it to daily activities.

Strategies

1. Go over any setbacks (or "almost setbacks") experienced since the last therapy session by the patient. Ask: What went through your mind when you did not do something more effective to avoid the setback? What more effective thoughts, actions, words, could you have used in order to avoid the setback?

   Then rehearse mentally with the patient a foreseeable situation in the near future by, first, asking the patient to imagine it vividly and to let the mental movie of the events roll while s/he gets in touch with all the feelings, good and bad, that this situation triggers. Second, guide the patient to visualize and experience vividly in his/her own mind the same situation, but now thinking, feeling, and acting in the best possible way. Third, repeat this so that patient feels more certain about her/his reaction to a stressful situation that, otherwise, could have been a setback.
2. Introduce and practice BRIMS. To introduce it, explain to

the patient that to permanently avoid any problems of adjustment in the future, s/he needs a method useful to control her mental reactions. This mind exercise uses a completely natural approach to controlling the thoughts that one allows in one's head. BRIMS stands for *B*reathing, *R*elaxation, *I*magery, *M*essages one gives oneself and *S*ign used to reactivate the benefits of this mind exercise.

In order to benefit from BRIMS one needs about half an hour of isolated time without distractions or interruptions. The imagery is practically what the patient did in strategy 2, immediately above. The messages of the fourth step in BRIMS consist of true and positive, encouraging statements that the person repeats to self slowly while being in a relaxed and concentrated state.

The following is a skeletal script which you may embellish as you see fit to be useful for your patient. Remember not to use commands ("You will") but realistic possibilities ("You are able"). Speak slowly, calmly, conveying a sense of peace and relaxation. Leave some short silences between sentences, allowing the patient to absorb what you are communicating to his/her innermost mind.

"Start by paying attention to your breathing. Allow your body to breathe on its best rhythm. Take your time to discover something you didn't realize before about your breathing. For instance, how does the air feel going through your nostrils? Or what happens in that split second when you stop inhaling and start exhaling? Become one with your breathing and connect breathing in with life, energy, and power. Think of exhaling as getting rid of negative thoughts, self-imposed limitations, unnecessary fears and doubts. Breathing in good things. Breathing out all the things you don't need." (Keep this type of chatter longer if you realize that your patient is still not breathing in a relaxed way).

"Continuing to breathe in a comfortable way, notice how your body is reacting to this type of breathing. All the systems in your body are starting to slow down and to relax. Imagine your muscles becoming less and less tense with every breath you take. More and more comfortable, relaxed, soft. And with it, a fresh sense of health and well-being, all over, from head to toes.

"Check now if you already notice one part of your body more relaxed than the rest. Any small part at all–toes, fingers, thighs. Which part is it? Now focus on that part that is more relaxed than the rest of your body and center your breathing on it. With every breath, feel that the relaxation starts to expand a little bit. Where does it go? To the right? To the left? Deeper into your body? Notice what is happening this very moment and enjoy the experience of your body following your mind. Your thoughts affect your body and you are learning to use your mind to benefit your body, to benefit yourself. Let the relaxation slowly move throughout your body as if you were nicely soaked in it. Completely. Comfortably soaked in this wonderful relaxation. Every breath increasing your well-being.

"Now you can imagine a 10-point scale. Look at it clearly in your mind's eye. The highest number tells you the highest level of relaxation you can reach. Zero is the number for the regular tension you use when you go about doing all the things you have to do. Now, paying attention to your scale: Is it horizontal or is it vertical? Is it round or is it a semicircle? Check what number pops up. What number is it?" (If the number reported is five or higher, proceed to the next step. If the number is four or lower, spend a little more time in the first two steps of BRIMS.)

"Your thoughts have relaxed you. The body follows the mind. You have proven to yourself that your thoughts make a difference. Feel good about it while still breathing for relaxation and inner calm.

"Now you can remember a situation in your life that you want to handle better than you do. By preparing yourself mentally to handle it well, to your complete satisfaction, you'll be ready to do so. Let that scene appear very sharply in your mind's eye. Make the scene real in your mental perception. Now, put yourself in it. Let it develop and get into it, experiencing the feelings fully. You are there going through it and doing it better than ever before. You feel great about your attitude, your behaviors, your way of handling it. Get into all the details: people involved, words exchanged, what you see, what you hear, what you notice. As the situation progresses, you feel even better about yourself until the whole thing ends.

"And while you are going through it, you can say to yourself, 'Yes, I'm doing it right this time. I'm proud of myself because this is me. I can do it and I feel terrific about it.' And linger on your positive feelings about what you are doing, now in your mind, to be ready when you have to do in your life, when you want to do it in your ordinary reality. You're doing it now. When the time comes to do it in reality, it'll be like repeating what you are familiar with.

"Still breathing gently and rhythmically, look at the 10-point scale once more. The original number may have changed. Keep the new number in mind so you know how well you're doing.

"Before returning to the ordinary mental channel, promise yourself that you'll practice the BRIMS exercise every day for the next month, so you get to really master this technique of self-therapy.

"To end, give yourself a sign that will be connected with your new success mind-set. The sign is to simply press together lightly your thumb and index finger of your nondominant hand. Every time you do this, your inner mind can activate your healthy mind-set. Do it now, gently pressing thumb and index finger to intensify your new, positive mind-set. Imagine it happening. Your fingers connect and they act like a switch that activates all your inner resources of success, health, and positiveness in your brain."

Prescription

1. Daily practice of BRIMS, keeping a written record. If patient misses one day, s/he will practice twice the following day or the next weekend.

Emphasize the need to make a commitment to master this technique of self-therapy in order to continue doing well without formal psychotherapy.

2. Schedule the last appointment for at least one month from this session.

Eighth Session

Objectives

1. Solidify gains made.
2. Terminate formal therapy.

Strategies

1. Review, in general, how patient is adjusting now to the original psychosocial stressor and, in general, to other life situations.
2. Review patient's practice of BRIMS and, if need be, lead patient through it once more, following the script proposed in the last session.
3. Arrange for possible telephone follow-up in three months and make specific "appointment" for patient to call you.
4. Depending on the patient and his/her situation, discuss possibility of patient joining a support group.
5. Explain in as positive and truthful terms as you can why you believe that therapy is concluded and completed.

Prescription

1. Continue practice of BRIMS every day.
2. With the help of the patient, find "stations" during the day in order to activate the success mind-set by means of the thumb and index finger sign. These stations can be, for instance, every time patient sees a Stop sign, or each time patient goes to the bathroom, and so on.

It is obvious that the eight sessions outlined in this chapter are only suggestions to guide you, the clinician, in the Solution-Oriented Brief Therapy (SOBT) approach. This is especially the case if you, like so many mental health practitioners, are not quite comfortable with this method. After practicing SOBT for a while and being reinforced by success, you'll develop your own unique style of practice within the general SOBT model.

In any case, the eight sessions will be modified by you according to the needs of your patient. The next chapter will provide you with techniques and ideas you may find useful to treat AD.

8

Teaching Patients Self-Therapy

All good therapists try to empower patients so that they are able to handle their life situations by themselves. Even so, the concept of self-therapy is not popular in the field of psychotherapy. Nevertheless, though new in psychotherapy, it is old in the business world. Here, authors like Dale Carnegie (1944), Norman Vincent Peale (1974), David Schwartz (1959), W. Clement Stone (1962), to mention just a few of the best known, have been teaching self-therapy without using this description for several decades. Their books, very popular in the corporate and general culture, have done much good for many.

More recently, Korn and Pratt (1987), Albert (1991), Bleck (1993), Araoz and Sutton (1994), and Kushel (1994), all of them psychotherapists by training, have also published self-therapy books. Moreover, the recovery movement has come out with literally hundreds of self-help books in the last few years, many of them excellent. The psychotherapy community as a whole has been rather critical of these books, claiming that they are too general, are not aimed at specific diagnoses, and often misdirect people into believing that they do not need psychotherapy. A few exceptions to this general trend (see Ellis, 1986) have integrated bibliotherapy with traditional psychotherapy. Self-therapy, for us, comes only after regular therapy and is no substitute for it.

This chapter proposes many methods and techniques that the mental health practitioner can pass on to patients afflicted by AD.

The general nature of these self-therapy practices is cognitive-behavioral: attitudes to change and actions to take. We offer them to you as a smorgasbord for you to pick and choose when involving the patient in her/his recovery.

THE HIDDEN SYMPTOM

Whatever the problem is, patients will benefit by becoming aware of how they are reacting to it. What are they saying to themselves about the symptoms? What mental images are they allowing in their mind to make things more difficult by their focusing on the negative, painful, limiting, or disabling aspects of the problem?

Patients will always benefit by realizing that they engage in this type of mental activity and by making an effort to find something less negative to think about rather than adding to their misery by focusing on it.

An important question to ask is whether the patient can truly admit that in spite of the symptoms there are good and positive things about his/her life that can become the focus of one's attention. If the patient refuses to recognize any of these truths, the therapist may help him/her pay attention to truisms that are taken for granted, such as the use of one's senses and mind.

Next, the patient has to be guided in order to start changing the focus of attention, from the negative and disabling to positive realities in his/her life. The expression used by many when something bad has happened, "It could have been worse," may help the patient to rejoice in the good things that are left, despite the psychosocial stressor experienced.

An example related to AD is that of Mr. D., from Chapter 2. He was impressed by the fact that one of the first things the therapist asked him was, "What comes to mind when you think of your problem?" After his retirement, to which Mr. D. had been looking forward with great expectations, he experienced a severe letdown. He was not aware of the fact that he was making things worse by his own pessimistic thinking ("This is what retirement is all about. I hate all this worrying," etc.) and by the mental images that he allowed and even fostered when he was feeling down (being sick, in a hospital or in an old folks home; his wife dying and his being all alone in Florida, away from children and grandchildren, etc.). Even though Mr. D. had been very opposed to going for psychotherapy, the mere fact that Dr. Y., his therapist, had started with this question changed his mind about therapy.

Often, as in the case of Mr. D., just to be aware of what one is doing mentally to oneself changes the negative self-hypnosis dramatically. We like to call it negative self-hypnosis because, like regular hypnosis, it connects with the inner mind or unconscious, bypassing the critical, logical functions of the brain. Thus, it causes damage to the individual (see Araoz, 1985) because the content of the messages is negative and self-defeating.

In practice, then, the clinician can, first, make the patient aware of the hidden symptom or negative self-hypnosis. Second, help the patient find other true and positive realities in his/her life and work on acceptable statements and related positive mental imagery. Third, guide the patient through the mental practice of psychovisualization so that an inner substitution takes place, moving from the hidden symptom to the more positive realities s/he needs to focus on. Fourth, and very important, insist on the benefits of repeating this mind exercise regularly until the negative thoughts have practically disappeared.

Personality Parts

When patients complain about their symptoms, which means very early in treatment, the clinician can point out that, as the body has many parts, so too does our personality. If the person says something like, "I can't believe that I am so stupid," the answer can introduce this concept. The clinician may say, "Yes, probably there is a stupid part in you. But this is only a part of you. You know that there is also a very smart part in you." (Ask the patient to think of recent situations when this part showed up.) "So, now, think of you in your stupid part. Try to concentrate and imagine how you look in your stupid part. How old are you? What are you doing? Where are you? Anybody with you? Who? What role does that person have in bringing up the stupid part of you?" Many more questions and interventions could be appropriate. The goal is to help the patient identify with that part of his personality.

The next step is to do the same with the smart part. Once patients have identified with the smart part, so that they can recognize experientially that both sides are parts of them, they are ready to work with this concept. Here you must encourage patients to engage in a cartoon-like way of thinking. To avoid confusion and distractions, ask them to do this with eyes closed and invite them to spend a moment relaxing by breathing slowly and rhythmically before getting in touch with the parts. Ask them to let the two parts talk about the problem or symptoms while another part is watching, listening, and evaluating.

This healthy form of personality splitting is especially useful with AD patients. One part is overreacting to the psychosocial stressor, while another part is conscious of the fact that it is an overreaction and has sought therapy because of it. The healthy part can talk to the overreacting part, tell it what to do and not to do.

This technique is often beneficial when people are ambivalent about decisions made or to be made. They are encouraged to identify the decision making part and to vividly imagine that part in their mind. Then to do the same with the doubting part. And finally, in the same cartoon-like fashion used before, get the two parts to talk to each other until they come to a resolution. It is productive to ask, while the patient is going through this inner discussion, "Which part do you want to take over? Which part are you going to allow to run your life at this point in time?"

The benefits of this approach are, first, that the person feels less helpless than before: Yes, there is a part in me that is not helpless or sick or whatever. Second, the person can take constructive measures to improve his/her life with the help of the stronger or healthier part inside. Finally, the therapist can refer to the negative part in the future if there are setbacks or other problems, thus showing an alliance with the healthier part and role modeling this attitude for the patient. This is what psychoanalysts refer to as the therapeutic alliance and which we do, not intellectually but experientially.

MAKE DREAMS COME TRUE

Early in the treatment process this technique gives patients a strong sense of hope to change and improve, since one of the typical traits of patients with AD is a sad and angry surprise at their own "failure." This method consists of asking patients to stop for a moment their concentration on the problem and symptoms and to focus their full attention on the future, when the problem is resolved and has become a thing of the past. Once patients indicate that they are paying attention to the time in the future, beyond the problem, you encourage them to observe very slowly every little detail of that mental scene: where they are, what they are doing, with whom are they, how are they feeling now, what thoughts and feelings do they have about the problem that was plaguing them some time ago, etc.

The purpose of this mind practice is to help patients become so familiar with the reality of their recovery that they make a more total commitment to move in that direction. This commitment has to be translated into practical actions to be taken as of today and the clinician must help patients make definite decisions about concrete things to do. Once patients come up with something constructive to do or to avoid, the professional invites them to visualize it for a few moments, paying attention to any inner voice that may try to sabotage the good intentions.

For this reason, the practice under your guidance must be slow but thorough, insisting that patients "be there" in their mind, and that they pay close attention to the feelings of success, pride, accomplishment, and happiness. In this case, it is also imperative to prescribe the frequent practice of this exercise at home and the strict recordkeeping of both the mental practice and the new behaviors that patients have decided to perform.

When we deal with AD, our experience shows that *To Make Dreams Come True* accelerates the process of healing and recovery. By means of this exercise, patients are forced to "distract" themselves from the problem, on which they have been unduly focused. And because the emphasis is on the positive feelings generated by the right actions, patients become further motivated to change.

MENTAL REHEARSAL

Related to the previous mind practice, *Mental Rehearsal* is very effective when patients find themselves "wanting" to do something that they are not actually doing. In AD patients, it is common to find that they make resolutions not to react in a particular, dysfunctional way. Yet they end up doing it regardless of their serious resolve. What to do then? Not to continue working on willpower, since this is obviously not producing results, but to go experientially. Patients are instructed to "see" themselves doing what has been resolved. This has to be done in great detail, step by step, considering all the circumstances, distractions, and interferences.

The husband who had retired and found it difficult to adjust to his new situation came to therapy complaining that he was frequently mean and nasty, without provocation, to his wife who was still working regular hours. He had tried to be nice, respectful, thoughtful, and patient, but in the last two or three months he inevitably got into a fight with her every single evening shortly after she arrived home from work. He realized that he needed more than just good intentions and accepted the suggestion that he mentally rehearse the behaviors he wanted to practice with his wife. He actually rehearsed in his mind, as if he were doing it in reality, to put himself in a good mood, to think lovingly of his wife, to recall good and pleasant scenes from their recent past. Then he continued mentally rehearsing how to greet her, smiling, kissing her, taking her coat, asking her how her day was, whether she wanted a drink or a cup of tea, and so on, in great detail. He continued this mind activity through dinner with his wife, watching television, and going to bed. He did this, first, with the clinician during the session and then at home many times since he had many free hours to engage in this rehearsal.

When this alone did not work, he realized that he had to mentally rehearse how to react to the things his wife did that irritated him, such as certain words she used, interruptions when he was talking, questions she asked that he considered "ridiculous and shallow," changing from subject to subject, and interrupting a conversation or whatever they were doing to answer the phone and engage in a prolonged conversation with one of her friends.

He realized that he had to mentally rehearse how to react less negatively to all these things that bothered him in his wife's behavior. He did so, over and over again, not trying to cover too much each time, but taking a single item at each mental rehearsal session.

After five days of working doggedly at it, he finally felt triumphant. He was so involved in the good, loving feelings towards his wife that her behavior did not bother him as before. He was looking forward to seeing his wife at the end of the day. And he knew what to expect, respecting her personality and the differences between him and her. He had learned to value so much the good things about his wife that the actions and things that bothered him before became minor and unimportant in his mind. *Mental Rehearsal* had made it possible for him to center on the foundation of love he had for his wife so that he could tolerate–though not like–the behaviors that had formerly led him to act in a way that he later regretted.

The patient now felt that this newly learned mental practice would be helpful in other areas of his life, such as becoming more active during retirement. He realized, intellectually, that now, having so much time on his hands, he could do many of the things that he had wanted to do for many years and was not doing. But the intellectual conviction alone did not help him. *Mental Rehearsal* was helpful to him in this area as it had been in his relationship with his wife.

This case is a good illustration of how AD patients can be assisted by *Mental Rehearsal.* The one thing for clinicians to keep in mind is that patients have to be aware of all the variables involved. The case just described did poorly in effecting change at first, in spite of the great care the patient had taken in mentally rehearsing how to act. It became meaningful only when he focused on his wife's behaviors that annoyed him. Only when he prepared himself, through *Mental Rehearsal,* to react differently–more positively–to those behaviors was he able to effect change in his own reactive behaviors. Because of the usefulness of *Mental Rehearsal,* this technique should be kept in mind when patients seem to be stuck, unable to move forward.

SOMATIC BRIDGE

This technique uses the body, what we feel, in order to decipher what is happening inside of ourselves. Often people who suffer from AD report somatic changes. It may range from a general awareness related to "feeling tired all the time" to more specific somatic awareness, such as unfamiliar pains in the legs (or arms or stomach or any other area of the body). This technique respects and takes seriously these symptoms, but theorizes that they *may* convey a message that needs to be translated into our current language of understanding. In other words, the somatic awareness must be decoded.

The patient is invited to be fully in touch with the symptom. It may be pain, discomfort, or merely greater awareness of an area of the body. Concentrating on this body awareness, any images, memories, feelings, or sensations that may seem unrelated to the initial awareness are allowed to come up. How is this done? By relaxing and focusing one's attention on the original sensation. The patient is prompted to try a metaphorical analogue or comparison, e.g., this discomfort is like a pressure on my side, like a fluid flowing inside of me, or the like. Once the patient "clicks" with one of these comparisons, s/he is instructed to visualize the pressure, the fluid, or whatever. Once that image appears, the patient tries to make it very vivid and sharp, capturing its size and color, its smell and sound, its weight and structure, etc. Then, the patient asks him/herself, "Is there a message from my inner mind here? If the discomfort is here and it appears to me like a fluid or pressure or whatever, it may come as message from my inner mind." Still relaxing, the person is asked to give it a little time before concluding the practice. If nothing comes up as a message, the patient can suggest to himself/herself that a dream tonight or in the next few days, or a passing mental flash when s/he is not thinking of any particular thing, may convey the message.

Since this practice has several steps, a summary of *Somatic Bridge* may be helpful. First, invite patients to relax by breathing slowly and associating exhaling with emptying the mind, until there is a noticeable feeling of relaxation. Second, ask patients to be fully aware of any bodily sensation. Third, tell them to allow any mental images, feelings, memories or other sensations to come up. For this to happen, patients should keep the relaxation through slow breathing while focusing on the original sensation. Fourth, ask them to use a comparison: "This pain is like..." If nothing comes up spontaneously, you suggest possibilities. Fifth, once patients find a metaphor or accept one of yours, request that they discover all its attributes, involving as many inner senses as possible. Take your time if a patient needs to go slowly. Sixth, "Is there a message here?"

Somatic Bridge helps patients to achieve a greater integration of mind and body, to trust the inner mind whose function is to help them (see Epstein, 1994) and to be, perhaps, more aware of personal reasons for their AD symptoms.

PAST ACCOMPLISHMENTS

Since the great majority of patients can truly admit to some past successes, by means of this technique you can help your patients to draw on past experiences for their current benefit. Among the important mental skills that all of us have used to succeed in the past, we can count attitude, perception, and projection. AD patients need the conviction that the thoughts they choose make a difference in the way they feel. For this, we need to teach them how to vividly review past accomplishments, as if these were taking place all over again in the present. They know that they have done and experienced those successful things. By reliving them now, they get back in touch with their pride, well-being, joy, and other energizing and empowering feelings that were real in the past. In owning these positive feelings, they bring them back to the present where they are essential to enable them to cope better with the psychosocial event or circumstances that have elicited so much stress as to produce behavioral impairment. They, therefore, build on precedent, not on wishful thinking. It can be done in two similar though different ways: first, by reliving any past accomplishment; second, by reliving a past accomplishment similar to the current stressful situation.

In the first case, the patient can recapture inner resources such as attitude, values, and ways of perceiving and reacting that were used in the past for something completely different, but that can be of help in any stressful set of circumstances. From a vivid reliving of a past successful situation, a connection is established with the present. Patients ask themselves what they can learn from that past success that applies to the current happening. Some of the same attitudes and some of the actions taken then may be useful now with some modification. Give patients time to review gently but thoroughly how they can help themselves now with the successful experience of the past. Perhaps they can view the past success as a training or dress rehearsal for the success that is waiting just around the corner. You emphasize, "You did it before. You can do it again now."

The second way of using *Past Accomplishments* is also possible with most clients. With a little help from the therapist, they can usually find some set of circumstances in the past that is at least remotely similar to the present situation. Then, staying with the similarities and how successfully that situation was resolved, the patient is helped as in the first instance just described.

Many AD patients use inner overstatements, the catastrophizing described by the RET therapists. In so doing, they seem to forget how well they may have coped with difficult situations in the past. This practice helps them focus on true past accomplishments so that they can draw from them to improve the current difficulties they are going through. The result is often a change in attitude, a new sense of hope, and a practical resolve to engage in more effective thinking and acting.

ROLE MODEL

This technique utilizes a common experience of many people. We admire and consider some human beings superior to the rest, heroes, people to imitate, role models. They may be historical characters or people we have known or even be close to. They are either actors or politicians, public figures or unknown people. Whoever they are, for each one of us one of these persons is a role model and a hero, if not in every respect, in many.

Role Model encourages patients to visualize their role model and to imagine him/her in the same situation that the patients find themselves. Vividly and clearly, watch the role model behave and act in the difficult situation, enter his/her inner mind and observe his/her mood, feelings, attitudes, etc. After a moment of this contemplation, patients imagine the role model talking to them, encouraging, supporting, understanding, but, at the same time, demanding better functioning and performance.

AD patients often start to believe that their situation is unique, impossible, the worst that anyone can imagine, and so on, adding the worse to the bad. A mental look at one's hero and role model often starts to make a difference and gives the patient new strength, changing his/her attitude and stance towards the horrible events of the current situation.

A man who had lost a great fortune in real estate came to therapy with suicidal thoughts and many symptoms of anxiety with some obsessive-compulsive manifestations. Asked to name some of the people he admired and respected as heroes and role models, he mentioned Theodore Roosevelt. He was directed to imagine himself at a private conference with Teddy Roosevelt. During this tête-à-tête, he told Teddy about his misfortune and heard in his mind the hero's reply, admonition, and advice. The patient was encouraged to repeat this "visit" with his hero until he could do exactly what Mr. Roosevelt told him to do.

The same man who had come to therapy talking about suicide was making serious plans two weeks later to rebuild his fortune. Through his imaginative use of Teddy Roosevelt, he had reached inner mental resources that were not used when he was concentrating on the financial disaster to which he had to adjust. The man he had admired for many years because of his values, spirit, and character served as a mirror for his better self and put him in contact with strengths and energy that he had neglected before.

All these cognitive, imaginative techniques that we are offering for your choice in teaching patients self-therapy should be used with great flexibility. Because of this, we purposely presented this clinical vignette of a patient who did not "see" in his mind's eye his hero in the same situation that he finds himself, behaving in an ideal manner, feeling confident and hopeful, and so on. This patient had a "mental conversation" with Teddy Roosevelt and through this metaphor of the hero activated inner resources that he had thus far neglected but that, in truth, he had always possessed. This is an example of that flexibility that the clinician needs to keep so as to be creatively individualized in the therapeutic work.

These cognitive techniques of self-therapy, more so than the next group of behavioral ones, work best when the clinician guides the patient through the technique and then, after having practiced it together in the office, prescribes it to the patient.

MENTAL SELF DEFENSE

Some of the Oriental forms of self defense use the energy and force of the opponent to reject their attacks. One can learn to do this mentally and the process is rather simple, but it requires practice, like all these mental techniques of self-therapy.

Mental Self Defense consists of mentally living the situation that upsets me and then using it to remind myself of the way I want to be. This "reminder" is done experientially, by means of vivid visualization. In other words, the upsetting situation acts as a trigger to start me thinking, feeling, and experiencing the right way (for me!) to conduct myself in it. By repeating this practice, I will get to the point where this happens without my thinking. The stressful event triggers peaceful and calm reactions on my part. Many AD patients convince themselves that they are at the mercy of the event that "created" the problem. By means of this technique, they convince themselves that they can control their life better.

Warner, a master carpenter for several Broadway shows with many years of experience, was forced to accept an early retirement at the age of 52. After consulting with lawyers, he realized there was nothing that he could do. He was angry and experienced many physical symptoms, such as diarrhea, heart palpitations, and shortness of breath. After seeking medical attention, he accepted the fact that he needed psychological assistance. By practicing *Mental Self Defense*, he got to the point where the details of his forced resignation, which had triggered anger, frustration, anxiety, and stress, started to do the opposite. Now he could bring these memories up and feel motivated to fill his life with other things, both professional and entertaining. Thanks to this practice, he was able to start planning his future. He became a teacher of carpentry in a large apprenticeship program run by his union and he found much more time to engage in fun things, such as playing golf and fishing, for which he had had very little time when he was working on Broadway.

Some have difficulty changing the mental connection from negative feelings about the stressful event to good feelings. For this to succeed, patients have to do some cognitive work before they get into the experiential practice described here. The cognitive work entails finding rational arguments and points of view that help one perceive the situation as bad but not catastrophic. Once this is done and the person is convinced that this event is not the end of the world for him/her, the experiential work of *Mental Self Defense* will be effective, as in the case of Warner.

COLOR BREATHING

This mind exercise is adapted from Napier (1990) and was learned by the senior author at one of her professional workshops. The AD patient must first have a fairly clear picture of the way one can be in spite of the psychosocial stressor; how one can feel, react, and think; how one can enjoy life and interact with family and friends despite the difficult situation one is going through. This image should be the goal of this exercise.

Then, in a relaxed position and mind set, trusting one's inner mind, the patient wonders what color would be appropriate for this mental picture. The color must be allowed to come to one's awareness, uncritically, spontaneously, from one's inner mind. Then one imagines this color in front of oneself. It may appear in unexpected ways: like a light or mist of water, etc. The next step is to connect the color with one's breathing; as one breathes, one thinks of breathing in this color that represents the goal or objective one wants to attain. In this case, the color represents a good adjustment. The breathing should be slowed down so that when one has inhaled, one can say to oneself, “I am capable of enjoying life in spite of this tribulation,” or a similar statement. This will act as a powerful self-suggestion, especially if one repeats it often during the day.

At exhalation, one imagines the color flowing through the body into the external world, preparing oneself for the enjoyment of life and the fulfillment of one’s goals regardless of the events that are taking place around oneself. This breathing practice is repeated a few times and at about the fifth time one focuses more acutely on the vivid image of what one wants to attain. In this case, the image portrays oneself successfully functioning and enjoying life despite the stresses that started the behavioral impairment of AD. This, too, must be repeated a couple of times before one returns to the ordinary way of using one’s mind.

The following summary of *Color Breathing* may make it easier to practice. The eight steps are as follows. First, ask the patient to give you a positive description of the way s/he can improve regarding the AD. This constructive and realistically positive mental picture is the goal of this exercise. Second, settling into a relaxed position and mind-set to ask oneself, “What color does this picture have,” allowing any color or combination of colors to come to awareness. Third, imagine this color in front of oneself. Fourth, connect the color with one’s breathing, taking it in when inhaling, filling oneself with the color. Fifth, as one inhales slowly, one gives oneself a constructive suggestion regarding one’s reaction to the stressor. Repeat this a few times. Sixth, concentrate on the breathing out, imagining the color coming out of all one’s pores, coloring the world, which had previously produced negative feelings, so that one can enjoy it even with the stressor. Repeat this a few times. Seventh, add now a vivid visualization of oneself acting, feeling, functioning in mind and body, successfully, happily, and with pride amidst the negative circumstances. Repeat a few times. Eight, return to the ordinary way of using one’s mind.

Melissa was a very educated, intellectual and mature patient who at the age of 50 lost her campaign for public office in her city. She came for psychotherapy, complaining that she should accept the defeat and not be so humiliated and embarrassed by it. She tried several mind exercises but stayed too cerebral, intellectualizing and criticizing them. With trepidation, the therapist tried *Color Breathing*, but Melissa, after an initial resistance, got into it wholeheartedly. The color that came to her awareness was bright, electric yellow. She found it very suitable for what she knew intellectually she wanted to do next, after her political defeat. The self-suggestion she used was encouraging to her: "You gave it a good try. Now you know, this is not for you. Go back to your university career, which you have enjoyed for many years." The color was attractive to her and started to color her thinking, as she put it, to the point that she was able to joke about her aborted political career. She was now happy that this defeat had given her a chance to return to the life she loved and to avoid all the headaches that being a political figure would have brought.

The paradox with Melissa was that her therapist believed that she, as an intellectual, would reject this type of metaphorical practice. The patient commented later that it had given her a new way of thinking about events; that her morose reaction to the defeat had, indeed, colored her view of it and that this practice had given her a powerful mental tool to change the color of things, not just in her case of AD but in many other areas of her life.

We have found that this practice becomes especially meaningful if we spend a little time emphasizing the advantage of trusting one's unconscious, which for us refers to the cognitive, benign unconscious studied by Epstein (1994).

The rest of this chapter will cover several behavioral self-therapy techniques; the ones listed so far are cognitive-experiential. Both are important in the program of self-therapy that the clinician should teach patients with AD. A serious commitment to change is imperative, with patients taking control of their life and assuming responsibility for their destiny. And the best way to change is to start changing. Voluntary change comes from doing things differently. Because change is often difficult and uncomfortable, we need as many techniques as we can find in order to start to change.

PRESCRIPTIONS

Chapter 7 shows many prescriptions that engage patients in their own change. The most behavioral of these are, among others, keeping a written record of one's daily performance of certain tasks and making a list of positive people and contacting them.

Many other prescriptions can be devised, such as forcing oneself to do things that one does not enjoy, like talking to someone boring and uninteresting, staying a bit longer in an unpleasant situation, doing something that one has been postponing for a while, and so forth.

The main value of prescriptions is that they give patients a sense of empowerment. They carry out the prescription and as a result they realize that they can do it. And if they can do this, chances are they can do other similar things, etc. Obviously, most people do not reason this out, but their experience of doing it is, in itself, convincing enough.

The most effective behavioral prescriptions are those that come from the patients themselves. When a clinician hears the common refrain, "I can't do it," s/he will help the patient by dissecting the "it." If the patient cannot do the whole thing, s/he may be able to do part of it or take the first steps that eventually may lead to the whole thing. In the case of AD, let's assume the patient is very unhappy about the new town where she moved to a couple of months ago because of career reasons. At that point she might say, "I'll never be able to like this damn town." The therapist may reply, "You may never like everything about the town. Is there anything at all that you like?" The patient may insist that there is absolutely nothing that she likes there. A patient-scored scale from "horrible" to "tolerable" may help. The therapist can point to several "tolerable" items and eventually the patient may admit that there are a few, albeit minor, things that are OK.

The behavioral prescription coming from this could be a list of other things that the patient likes about the new town–or, at least, things that the patient finds less dislikable. Another prescription originating from the same scenario is the possibility of writing a short story to highlight all the horrible things about the town. A third possibility is to ask the patient to find other people who dislike the town and establish a griping network, with their own newsletter, meetings, and other elements of organizations.

This is, then, the first rule for effective behavioral prescriptions: They come from what the patient is dealing with in her life and saying during the session. The other rule to keep in mind when giving behavioral prescriptions is that the task to be performed be concrete, uncomplicated, and doable. If an AD patient is reacting negatively to the new town, refusing to go out of the house, being unfriendly or distant to the town's people, becoming very critical of every custom and regulation in town, an effective prescription will certainly not encompass all of the above. The behavioral prescription will be limited to one of the items mentioned–to make the effort to visit different parts of town, or to be friendly to various residents, or to stop oneself from criticizing the town, even mentally. And a written record of performance should be kept.

The last rule for behavioral prescriptions is to establish consequences for lack of performance. In most cases, a discussion is enough to make the patient accept the fact that the agreement to do something in order to improve one's situation is a commitment to oneself. If one fails to do it, it is not OK and one has to make up for it in some way. Here, too, the patient should be involved in deciding what the consequences of missing out on a commitment should be. Frequently, the most simple consequence is for the patient who did not do what s/he was supposed to do on one particular day to commit to doing it twice the following day. Any semblance of punishment should be avoided for the most part. The factual approach is the best: If I don't do something that I agreed on doing, I can't just ignore the fact that I did not keep my word; I have to do it later.

The fourth rule is to have constant feedback. This is achieved by patients keeping a written record of their performance. The form provided (Figure 8.1) may be used for this purpose, with practically any type of behavioral prescription. Patients will benefit by keeping this record visible, on the refrigerator door or on the bathroom mirror, for example, so that they get constant feedback and have an inescapable reminder.

FIGURE 8.1

The Weekly Schedule Form

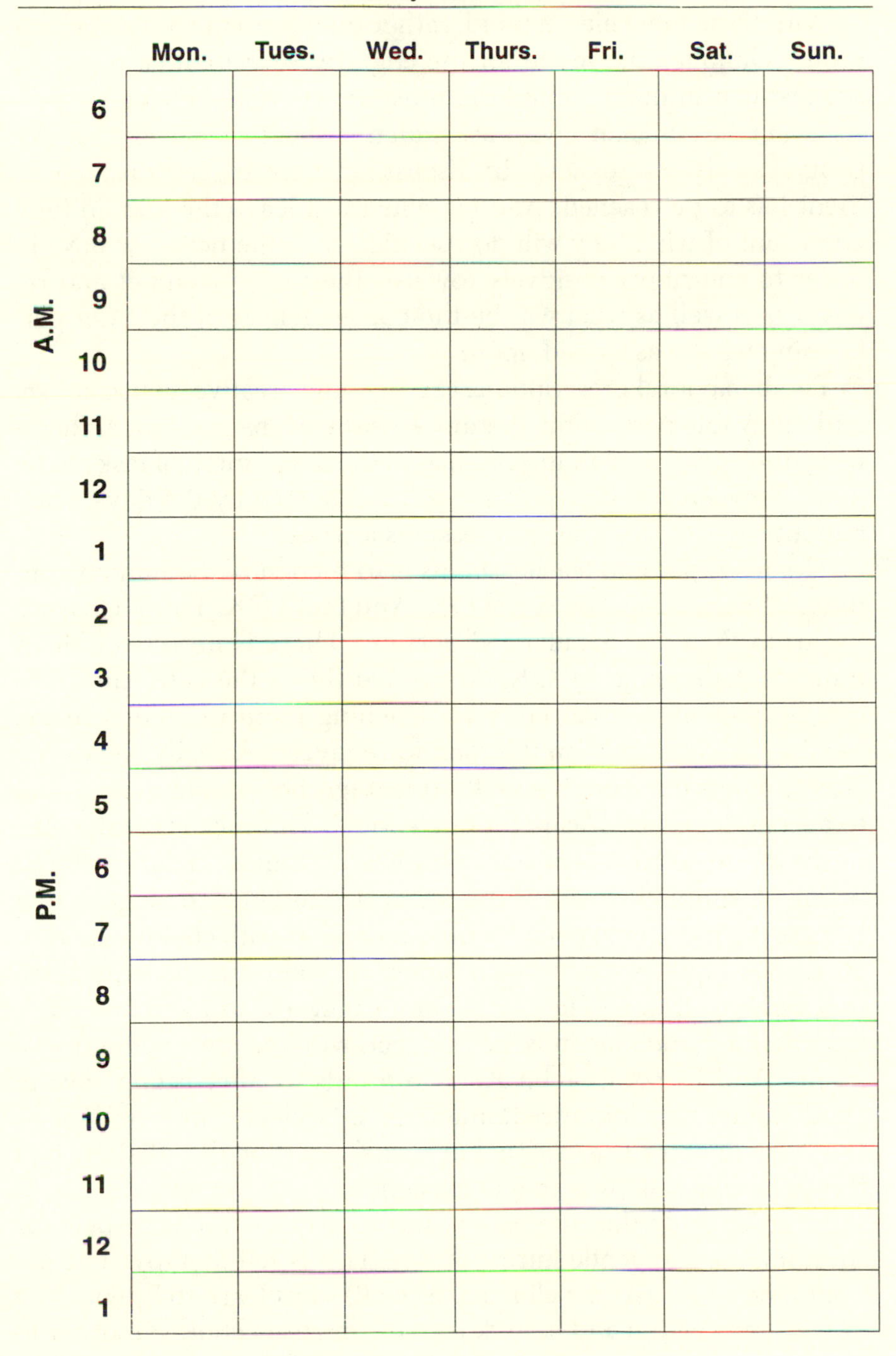

		Mon.	Tues.	Wed.	Thurs.	Fri.	Sat.	Sun.
A.M.	6							
	7							
	8							
	9							
	10							
	11							
	12							
	1							
	2							
	3							
	4							
	5							
P.M.	6							
	7							
	8							
	9							
	10							
	11							
	12							
	1							

With these four rules in mind, rather than present a list of behavioral techniques, as we did for the cognitive-experiential ones, we suggest that in order to find the most appropriate behavioral prescription the clinician always ask patients what they can do to make progress between sessions. In discussing these suggestions, agreement has to be reached. And patients must leave the session fully cognizant of what they will do specifically in the next few days in order to contribute positively towards their improvement and recovery, as well as what will be the consequences of their not performing what was agreed upon.

The behavioral prescriptions can become creative, constructive, and enjoyable parts of the therapy session. Many traditional therapists don't give enough importance to the assignment of tasks to be done between sessions, perhaps still influenced by the days when patients used to go to several sessions a week.

The main point to teach patients is to recognize the human condition: I'm not OK. You're not OK. And that's OK. This is closer to the truth than the popularized version. There is no other OK in humans than being *not* OK. And since this is the case, clinicians can do patients a great favor by teaching them to recognize the need to be constantly on the road to recovery. Actually, as Moore (1994) points out, cure is a myth. It is safer, better, and more joyful to accept the need to "care for one's soul." This means to take seriously the need to accept our complicated human nature without trying to simplify it with shortcuts and standardized slogans that bypass the individual person's uniqueness, or with choking materialism that equates having with being, or with unrealistic idealism that believes in a perfect world. The eagerness to overcome life's uncertainties and pain must be replaced with the raw experience of living. And living, as John Keats reminds us after listing several "bad" things that comprise human life, is "to feel existence." For us the wisdom of his *Endymion* lies in Keats' assertion that all these bad things are the only way to feel existence.

In order to do this, the patient has to acquire a new respect for mindfulness and gentle introspection. This is self-therapy! The patient (and obviously the clinician as well) must learn to listen to the voices from within and to look inside ("intro-spection") in order to benefit from previous "lessons" from one's history and experience through the years.

This process is never-ending and requires perseverance and a sense of adventure that is acquired by doing it. The more familiar we become with our inner self, the more excited we feel knowing that there is so much wealth and wisdom there that is ours. The item of "spirituality" that we added in Chapter 10 comprises these inner realities of being human, such as nobility, generosity, and transcending the familiar, the material, the known. Self-therapy is not a do-it-yourself trick, but genuine caring for one's inner self, for one's spiritual life. And this is what the clinician must teach the patient. This is true adjustment to living.

9

When Eight Sessions Are Not Enough

There are many reasons the clinician may need to request the managed care company in charge of a particular case to approve further treatment sessions. The reasons come from two valid sources: either the stressor that elicited the maladaptive reaction on the part of the patient or circumstances on the part of the patient. The first group of reasons range from lack of change in the *chronic* psychosocial stressor, to new stressors introduced in the picture of an initial *acute* stressor, to, finally, the cascading of stressors as a consequence of the initial *acute or chronic* stressor that elicited the patient's maladaptive reaction constituting the Adjustment Disorder.

The first category (no change in the *chronic* stressor), can be exemplified by the elderly widowed mother whose only son, for reasons unknown to her, refuses to have any contact with her, even though they live in the same town. The mother suspects the influence of the son's wife on this behavior, which started shortly before his wedding. The longer the situation continues, the more difficult it is for the mother to "adjust" to it, hope always remaining that "next time I try to contact him, things might be different."

New acute stressors may be introduced in the picture of the initial *acute* stressor. For instance, the man who is adjusting to a bladder cancer diagnosis learns that his pregnant daughter has lost the baby shortly before the due date.

Finally, the cascading of stressors may come as a consequence of an *acute* stressor, like in the preceding case, if the bladder cancer patient loses his job because of prolonged absenteeism and this new development leads to a devastating upset in his finances; he has to adjust to all new stressors.

This damaging effect of the accumulation of stressors may also come from an initial *chronic* one. In the case above, the mother may learn through indirect sources that her son is moving out of town. When she invites him to have lunch to say good bye, he reacts with anger, refusing to see her and to give her the phone number or the address of his new home. The chronic stressor becomes complicated with the new one related to the son's move, increasing the severity of the total situation to which the patient needs to adjust.

In all these cases, the clinician may need more than the initial sessions allotted by the managed care company to treat a patient with Adjustment Disorder. Presently, we shall discuss the most effective ways to proceed in order to benefit the patient by working collaboratively with the health maintenance organizations or HMOs. But before doing so, the other group of reasons mentioned above and justifying an extension of the initial eight sessions allotted to treat a person with AD have to be discussed. This is the issue of *patient resistance* to treatment and, in general, the total reaction of the patient to the treatment with all its components, especially the clinical methods used and the patient–therapist interaction and communication.

In the outline of eight treatment sessions in Chapter 7, we indicated several points, as early as the second session, at which the patient is confronted with the need to take responsibility for treatment. Unlike many medical procedures, psychotherapy demands much more than keeping appointments or taking medication several times a day. It requires *involvement* in the difficult process of change, the therapy session proper being only a landmark and checking point in that process.

Some Solution-Oriented Brief Therapy advocates seem to imply that resistance is a spurious construct, often if not always utilized to justify the clinician's incompetence. Yes, we agree that resistance has been used in that manner. But the old concept of resistance, key in Freud's thinking, is still valid today. Contradictory to the patient's conscious motivation, irrational and illogical in itself, there is resistance when the patient, for instance, after agreeing to do something conducive to his/her cure, well-being, and recovery, ends up not doing it for no good, justifiable reason at all. This is an obvious instance of resistance as a nonconscious behavior.

Obviously, there are many other forms of resistance. In all of them, one of the most powerful techniques available is the *activation of personality parts.* The clinician asks the patient to identify the *part* that agreed to follow a prescription or to be in therapy. After this personality part has been discovered by the same patient, the other *part* that found reasons and excuses not to follow the same prescription is now identified. Next, the two patient's personality parts are invited to engage in a conversation about what happened until the patient becomes fully aware of which personality part is influencing behavior and is, thus, controlling his/her life despite all conscious motivation.

Among the many authors who have dealt with the practical aspects of resistance and how to deal with it effectively in the clinical setting, Sherman, Oresky, and Rountree (1991) propose a *contracting-for-results strategy*, with three additional techniques and 32 suggestions for different types of resistance. What they discuss is directed at family therapy, but many of the ideas offer very practical use in any form of therapy, especially in the traditional one-to-one format.

Each clinician has a unique style of working and each must respect that style. The following cannot be used like a gimmick, without regard for the therapist's style. We have found that *to join the resistance*, when nothing else has worked, is often effective, though risky. Applying this to AD patients who have not shown real improvement after eight sessions, we may say something like the following in the hope that they may react against our expressed hopelessness and our suggestion that they accept the misery produced by the stressor since therapy has been unable to help them.

> Perhaps it was a mistake for you to want to change anything about this situation. (*The very conservative and traditional mother had recently learned that her 26-year-old youngest son, living across the country, had openly declared his homosexuality.*) It continues the same and the only thing you can change is your mind. But your efforts at that

> have failed too. I am thinking that I may have made a mistake, too, by trying to help you. I believe now that you have not mourned long enough and deep enough the loss of your son to normalcy, respectability, and decency. He *is* sick, despicable, and indecent. How can he do such a thing to you and your family?
>
> So, you must continue to feel miserable and accept this horrible burden from a horrible son for the rest of your life. This is the only thing that therapy can help you with: to accept being miserable and in pain forever.

Obviously, this is merely a sample of words and sentences. The important point is to capture the attitude and content of this strategy. Without mockery or sarcasm, the clinician joins the resistance and verbalizes an attitude of resignation and acceptance of it that comes from the frustration produced by the lack of success: Because you haven't changed, you cannot force yourself to change any longer and therefore you must forget about changing for the time being and learn to live with your dissatisfaction. If the patient responds by indicating that the therapy should continue to have the initial goal, the above-mentioned *personality parts* technique can be very useful, even if it had been employed previously without good results.

Regarding the most effective ways to proceed with the managed care companies in order to obtain authorization to prolong treatment past the original eight sessions, the words of Goodman et al. (1992) deserve to be quoted: "Obtaining authorization from reviewers for further treatment...is probably the most challenging and, at times vexing component of the external review process" (p. 119). Because of this, they warn the clinician against establishing an adversarial setting in negotiating the extension of services. For this, a factual approach is essential: a clear description of behaviors and how the patient still shows behavioral impairment, because of which s/he needs further therapy in order to increase the healthy, constructive, behaviors contradictory to impairment. Any other elements, whether showing emotionality or implying dreadful consequences for the patient or threat to the HMO's, are totally unwarranted. This "facts only" rule applies to both telephone conversations and written reports. In the long run, the latter are less time-consuming than telephone work.

For the written reports, the same authors provide us with a four-point method. First, list the patient's original therapeutic objectives and the behaviors by which the patient has shown the attainment of these or the progress towards these objectives. Second, give an updated treatment plan. Third, focus on the current patient behavioral impairment. Fourth, indicate concretely the need to continue treatment and the danger of not doing so in terms of probable risk of regressing to increased impairment, thus losing the gains made so far.

By including clear information on the patient's behaviors that show movement towards the therapeutic goals since the beginning of treatment (positive behaviors), as well as on the other behaviors showing the need for further progress and improvement (lacking behaviors), the clinical necessity for continuing treatment at this time is *factually* established.

To make this request for further treatment easier, it is always wise to leave the door open from the very beginning of treatment for additional therapeutic interventions or modifications in clinical procedures by stating explicitly two or three of these possible procedures in the initial report for the HMO's. A general statement such as, "Patient's progress will determine advisability of these interventions in future," prepares the managed care company and its reviewer for the possible request for more treatment time coming at the end of the eighth session.

Regarding the actual request to be sent (we already stated that it is more efficient to do it in writing rather than over the telephone), it should be centered on the patient's therapeutic goals, since "goals serve the important function of structuring the treatment in a positive direction," as Fox (1987, p. 495) stated succinctly. We find the language of the *Consolidated Standards Manual* (see Joint Commission on Accreditation of Healthcare Organizations, 1991) regarding goals and objectives a bit confusing. For instance, Standard PM.27 mandates "specific goals that the patient must achieve to attain, maintain and/or reestablish emotional and/or physical health as well as maximum growth and adaptive capabilities," whereas Standard PM.28 demands "specific objectives that relate to the goals...written in measurable terms and includ[ing] expected achievement dates. Therefore, this usage makes *goals* what has to be accomplished and *objectives* the concrete steps towards those goals and the probable time period to achieve them.

We wonder why the old distinction between long-term and short-term goals was abandoned. Serious Brief Therapy authors like de Shazer (1988) are very focused and goal-oriented without language complications. Another author, Fox (1987), makes a practical distinction between three types of goals: *Final, Facilitative*, and *Functional.* In other words, first, the long-term object or goal to be achieved is considered. Second, what needs to be done to achieve it is accepted and planned. And third, the concrete actions to be taken in the short term in order to achieve the long-term goal are decided upon.

For example, using the four vignettes from Chapter 4, Marc's goals for therapy are as follows. *Final* goal: To adapt constructively to the new situation forced by economic realities. *Facilitative* goal: Here the possibilities of filling his free time away from home effectively must be examined. Then choices must be made. During his free hours Marc could (a) take a course for his enjoyment or professional advancement, (b) learn a skill he might be interested in (a foreign language, playing a musical instrument, scuba diving, or the like), (c) practice a sport or hobby. He has to be helped to choose what he decides to do with his free time during the week away from home. *Functional* goal: Let's assume that he decides to join a bowling league. Now, he has to make concrete plans to call the bowling alley, register for a particular evening, and make up his mind that he'll show up and that he'll give it a good try even if the people in the league are not exactly "his type."

The request for further treatment sessions, if required, should concentrate on the patient's behavior, the more factual the better: what Marc has achieved thus far, according to the agreed upon goals, listed earlier. Let's suppose that he has joined the bowling league and has attended five times in eight weeks. Further, it must be stated that the three times that he missed he was drinking again, feeling sorry for himself, and giving into depression. In other words, Marc reverts to the "mixed disturbance of emotions and conduct" of the initial diagnosis. The conclusion of the above factual description of the patient's progress, as well as of his continued behavioral impairment, is that interruption of therapy at this point gives the clinician good reason to believe that Marc may give in more and more to the behavioral impairment that brought him to therapy and, therefore, that continuation of treatment is strongly advised.

In the case of Elizabeth, also from Chapter 4, and this time following de Shazer's (1988) thinking about the fact that "goals help to define how therapist and client alike can know that the problem is solved" (p. 97), the therapist must establish a way of measuring goal attainment. Therefore, the goals must be clear and the actions to take well understood. In de Shazer's (p. 95) metaphor, goals are targets that clinician and patient shoot for, while the tasks to perform in order to attain the goals are arrows. Therefore, the *goals* for this patient are: to be more relaxed; to feel better physically, diminishing her somatic symptoms; to spend more quality time with her husband. The *actions* to be taken are: watching her negative self-hypnosis so she can stop it; making time every day to relax in a methodic way (to be learned in therapy); using her imagination to leave all internship concerns outside her door when she returns home; arranging to have every week some fun activity with spouse; patiently starting to look for and find another job or to consider a more stringent budget as a temporary measure until she finishes her doctorate.

Therefore, the request for additional treatment sessions for Elizabeth will specify concretely and in as measurable a form as possible three items of information for the managed care company. These are, first, what she has already shown and accomplished in terms of goal attainment; second, what she still needs to do in this respect; and third, the rationale for the request regarding past, current, and predictable behavioral impairment. The report/request will include these or similar statements:

> Patient has already learned to relax in a naturalistic way by using her imagination. This has improved the domestic situation: There is less tension, more adult discussion of issues and disagreements, more time with husband every week doing some mutually enjoyable activity, avoidance of "shop talk" unless this is necessary or initiated by spouse. Patient has also experienced fewer somatic

symptoms most of the time. She attributes this to her mental practice of relaxation, which she has done practically every day. However, she still needs to have more control of her feelings about the stressor that precipitated her diagnostic condition of Adjustment Disorder. For this, she needs further relaxation practice.

Often, she experiences great stress in keeping a cheerful exterior, especially with her husband, while her mind is racing with intrusive thoughts related to her lost job. She is still not adept enough at the practice of relaxation, thought control, and creative imagination. Without treatment, stress will most probably continue to increase, with a consequent recurrence of the old symptomatology. Recommendation of, at least, four more treatment sessions is strongly advised. The new sessions will be used to build on her behavioral and attitudinal gains so far by progressively encouraging her to handle situations that previously triggered her symptoms of impairment; by continuing to monitor her practice of relaxation and creative imagination; and by teaching her new, effective techniques of self-therapy, such as Mental Rehearsal and Somatic Bridge. *(These techniques were explained in Chapter 8.)*

The important point in the above text is to center the request for further visits to continue treatment around the patient's goals for therapy. For the next case we purposely present the request for further treatment in outline form. Thus, with the last case and the next, we provide the clinician with different styles from which to choose for this important juncture in the treatment of a patient.

Ed, the person in the third vignette in Chapter 4, has felt mildly depressed since his lover informed him that he needed more freedom to see other men. He started questioning his life style, thinking that he would like to have children and worrying about his future. These feelings have made him anxious, nervous, insecure, and irritable. This is "the" problem: the reason for his seeking therapy at this time in his life. So, what is the solution for his problem? What does he want to gain from psychotherapy? What is his goal? Obviously, to feel better by making the right decisions. But this is too vague a goal for our purpose and we need to state it in concrete behavioral terms, in measurable form. Therefore, Ed's therapeutic goals may be put in these or similar terms:

Patient's goals:

1. To mourn the loss of a meaningful and long relationship just ended;
2. To decide about his life style in the future;
3. To consider a wider range of social options after having been overly involved in the gay community to the exclusion of other people.

But goals without a plan of action are useless at best. Consequently, the clinician must also outline what actions Ed should take and within what time frame. This additional piece of information for the managed care company responsible for Ed's case, may be stated as follows:

Patient's actions to attain his goals will be:

1. To give himself three months to accept the end of the last relationship by monitoring his thinking/self-talk;
2. To master practical ways of using techniques of creative imagination in order to replace negative self-hypnosis with constructive thoughts;
3. To inquire into diverse social activities around his interests and hobbies, regardless of who else is involved in these activities.

The above two paragraphs belong at the beginning of treatment and the request for further therapy sessions must be based on them. Thus, when informing the managed care company that Ed needs further treatment, the clinician may express, first, the goals that the treatment has helped the patient attain so far. Here is a possible statement:

In regards to his stated goals, the patient has made this progress so far:

1. He has learned to control his nervousness through cognitive/experiential techniques acquired and practiced in therapy;

2. He has accepted the inevitability of the end of his cherished relationship and feels free now to think of, and eventually to act on, a new relationship;
3. He has started to socialize with different classes of people by going regularly to places where he can meet them.

The next information item necessary for the health maintenance or managed care companies refers also to the original goals by indicating what still needs to be done in order to attain them completely. Therefore, given the very process of therapy and the progress made so far, this item may be formulated accordingly. Here is an example:

> Request for needed further treatment is based on the fact that patient still needs to engage in the following behaviors conducive to the attainment of his goals in order to make sure that his problem is solved:
>
> 1. To start accepting a change in life style as a possibility for himself, for which he still needs the support of therapy; patient still needs to learn and use cognitive techniques to fully effect this mind set switch;
> 2. To try new behaviors regarding heterosexual dating;
> 3. To mentally process heterosexual dating without negative feelings;
> 4. To accept fully his chosen self-definition as a heterosexual.

This is a good example of the new developments that take place in the course of psychotherapy. Ed did not enter treatment with the intention of changing his sexual identity, but rather because he was hurt by his lover's rejection. He wanted to resolve that hurt. However, in working on it, he realized that his wife's rejection had triggered his move towards a homosexual relationship without his having given himself enough time to think this out. Now, experiencing anew the hurt of rejection, he saw the need to think carefully before acting, as he had done four years earlier. He came to the conclusion that it was to his benefit to expose himself to further relationships with women in order to resolve his doubts about his sexual identity.

This changed the course of therapy, as the previous statements requesting further treatment sessions indicate.

It is the responsibility of the clinician to inform the managed care companies on the progress of treatment. S/he must insist when they, without clinical experience and perceiving therapy from a business perspective, object to the granting of further treatment sessions. Dealing with the complex and hardly predictable variables of human psychology, this type of treatment has to be open and flexible. Modifications, change in direction, unexpected new variables, and much more are *normal* in this work and the business mind behind managed care needs to be educated and constantly reminded of it by the clinicians who handle these cases.

In this spirit, the request for additional treatment sessions should be made. But because the managed care people are not clinicians, as we shall discuss in the Conclusion of this book, the mental health practitioner has to stand firm in the conviction that nobody can arbitrarily regulate the time and number of sessions that are appropriate for a particular individual in order to reach therapeutic goals. What is *average* for a specific condition or mental disorder is not necessarily what a particular patient will profit from. The clinician, as the professional responsible for the well-being of the patient, must defend the right of each patient to get the best service that the patient needs.

Thus, requesting further sessions to complete the right treatment that was begun and that has been so far successful is an obligation the clinician has when the case requires it. No attitude of begging and asking favors is in order here. What is needed is, rather, a courteous, firm, and professional stance in order to give the managed care people all the factual explanations they need to understand the reasons for the request. In this way, the clinician can enter into a cooperative relationship with those who hold the purse strings.

We have to assume that the clinician has been admitted to work with a particular managed care company to do a professional job. Part of that job is the request for further treatment with which this chapter has dealt.

10

Spirituality as a Factor in the Writing of Reports for Managed Care Corporations

This chapter will briefly go over practical points to keep in mind when writing reports for the different managed care companies. Many of them require periodical submissions of progress reports in order to grant permission for further treatment sessions. Because many mental health service providers have negative feelings about this practice, they do themselves and their patients a disservice by not spending enough attention, time, and energy in writing these reports.

By not submitting more accurately what the managed care companies request, they often create their own troubles; they don't satisfy the company's requirements and therefore have to rewrite the report or add important details to it, spending more time and giving themselves more "reasons" to complain about the system. The result of this oppositional attitude is that extended treatment is often denied, to the detriment of patients. Whether we like it or not, Lawrence Weed's (1969) prophesy more than two decades ago, has come true: "The *economic and organizational aspects of medical care*...will determine the quality and quantity of care they will be able to deliver" (p. 122) (our emphasis).

Managed care companies do control and determine the quality and quantity of care; practitioners will not help the cause or themselves by rebelling or doing a halfway job. We offer this chapter to help avoid the problem and to simplify the process for the practitioner.

In the same book just mentioned, Weed (1969) complained about the confusing, even messy, treatment records that would not allow "a medical teacher or member of an accrediting agency" to assess the quality of treatment administered. He was referring to records in all branches of medicine, not necessarily psychiatry. Because of the confusion and lack of clarity of the medical records in the late 1960s, the *Weed System* was created and popularized. This is a documentation system that provides the reasons for initiating patient care and for clearly displaying the rationale underlying the treatment decisions responsible for the progress of the case.

Building on the Weed System, Goodman et al. (1992) have developed a very useful and well thought out system specifically designed for mental health care. Their tome deserves a place on every psychotherapist's bookshelf. We summarize their system which, we believe, will become as respected in mental health care as the Weed System was in general medical care.

As mentioned in Chapter 3, the current challenge for the clinician is to describe what's wrong with the patient in impairment language, thus informing managed care companies of patients' behavioral dysfunctions in a form they can easily understand. In order to do this, the practitioner may use one of the two impairment models we offered in Chapter 3. They are useful for reporting on the patient's initial condition as well as on the progress of psychotherapy. Although the two forms provided there are basically sufficient for that purpose, the more detailed versions of them included here (Figures 10.1 and 10.2) may be more convenient for the clinician learning to work according to the stricter accountability of managed care.

Goodman et al. (1992) use a felicitous metaphor for impairment, calling it behavioral windows, allowing us to look into the patients' world in order to understand what's wrong with them. These windows also let us discover their inner resources to decide on the necessary means to be taken in order to correct the impairment.

THE ROLE OF SPIRITUALITY

To be specific and accurate in describing patient impairment, the Goodman et al. (1992) model considers four spheres, as reflected in

FIGURE 10.1

Patient Impairment Severity

Following the Goodman, Brown, & Deitz (1992) model

Patient:	**Date:**	
	Symptoms	**Severity***
Biopsychology	______________	___
	______________	___
	______________	___
Intimacy	______________	___
	______________	___
	______________	___
People Interaction	______________	___
	______________	___
	______________	___
Future Orientation	______________	___
	______________	___
	______________	___
Spirituality	______________	___
	______________	___
	______________	___

Notes: ______________________________

____

***Severity Level**

0 Absent
1 Moderate
2 Debilitating
3 Incapacitating
4 Dangerous!

FIGURE 10.2

Patient Impairment Severity

Following the Lazarus (1981) model

Patient: **Date:**

	Symptoms	Severity*
Behavior	________________	____
	________________	____
	________________	____
Affect	________________	____
	________________	____
	________________	____
Sensations	________________	____
	________________	____
	________________	____
Images	________________	____
	________________	____
	________________	____
Cognition	________________	____
	________________	____
	________________	____
Interpersonal	________________	____
	________________	____
	________________	____
Diet	________________	____
	________________	____
	________________	____

Notes: ________________________________

____

***Severity Level**

0 Absent
1 Moderate
2 Debilitating
3 Incapacitating
4 Dangerous!

the forms we propose, while the Lazarus (1981) model covers seven areas. To both models we like to add *spirituality* as a unique, separate, and humanly important item. It is true that spirituality can be subsumed, in the first model, at least under Biopsychology and Future Orientation, and in the Lazarus model under, at least, Behavior, Affect, Imagery, and Cognition, and even under the complete BASIC ID in many cases.

But precisely because of the confusion created by subsuming spirituality under other headings, which in many cases identifies it with religion or religiosity, and because of its importance, we suggest its addition to the two models.

By spirituality, we mean with Epstein and Brodsky (1993) a way of thinking about one's experience of living that transcends rational thinking. But, unlike him, we separate it sharply from religion, which we understand as only one of many possible manifestations of spirituality. Another, universal expression of spirituality that is both primitive and sophisticated is art in any form or through any medium. Spirituality means transcendence from our immediate sensory and rational reality or the ability to free oneself periodically from the material/temporal world. It is the partial renunciation of understanding in favor of experiencing what, without understanding, becomes mysterious and of the accepting of the unknown mystery.

More difficult than other areas of human functioning to pinpoint behaviorally, it does allow for a behavioral description nevertheless. Thus, a person who accepts with inner peace the fact that not every aspect of life is under one's control and who believes in the future, trusting what the process of life has in store for oneself, pleasant and unpleasant, is showing spirituality. Spirituality shows when most others despair and one does not; when most others are sure and one is not; when most others react predictably and one does not. To be at peace with uncertainty and the unknown, with the old that others discard and with the new that most fear, is a sign of spirituality.

In behaviorally reporting on this human trait, we suggest proceeding as in the other items, using different levels of impairment, as shown in the forms in this chapter. These levels we have taken from Chapter 6 of Goodman et al. (1992).

These authors did not reinvent the wheel on this issue of illness severity, but conducted a serious investigation of previous severity-of-illness systems. They masterfully adapted the concept to what they refer to as "mental healthcare treatment services" throughout their book, correctly believing that this concept is as relevant to our field as it is to medicine in general.

Severity refers to the importance of the symptoms. Are they serious enough to require immediate attention, care and treatment? Are they grave enough to warrant professional concern and worry? Some symptoms are definitely imminently dangerous to the welfare of the patient or to that of others close to him/her. Other symptoms are clearly incapacitating and handicapping. However, there are symptoms that are rather debilitating and limiting but not imminently dangerous or even incapacitating. Finally, there are moderate, mild, a-bit-more-serious-than-simple idiosyncrasies, symptoms.

In order to organize this important information for clinical action, Goodman et al. (1992) come up with five levels of severity of mental/behavioral problems. Level 0 indicates absence of severity, urgency and danger. Level 1 designates moderate severity. Level 2 is for symptoms that cause weakness and limitations in behavior. Level 3 shows behavior that is handicapping to the patient. The most severe, Level 4, indicates imminent and severe danger.

Therefore, when dealing with behavioral changes in the individual that are evidently life-threatening to him/her or to others, the clinical action to be taken is very different from when the symptoms are just a bit out of the ordinary.

The valid question about spirituality as an item to be considered by mental health practitioners is, Why is this important? We believe that this concept allows us to understand people's *beliefs*, as they affect *perception* of events, *interpretation* of reality, *projections* into the future, and *morality* in the broadest sense of what is right and wrong, even about recovering from the current behavioral impairment. The level of *stamina* (ego strength, willpower, inner resources, or whatever other designation we choose to use) is directly related to spirituality.

Profiles of Spirituality

Thus, when dealing with AD patients, the following spirituality profiles show significant differences for treatment.

Impairment: No meaning in his life and toying with suicidal ideation. The severity for this symptom is uncertain. Suicidal thoughts by themselves and out of the total context of personality do not have a precise diagnostic meaning. In this case, and because one considers spirituality, the suicidal ideation may be dangerous (Severity Level 4) because of the patient's lack of meaning in his life. But because the patient is merely "toying"' with these thoughts, they may be debilitating only (Severity Level 2).

In cases of uncertainty in any category, our advice is to be rather conservative. Uncertainty in the above case means that it has to be considered initially as if the severity were at Level 4. In the following sessions, the severity level may be downgraded.

Impairment: Irrationally convinced that God is punishing her with the loss of job and income. Rationally, she realizes that this thinking is absurd. Wishes she had a better philosophy of life. The severity for this impairment is between 2 and 1, since her beliefs compromise her functioning (Level 2); at the same time, her wish for a better philosophy of life seems amenable to repair (Level 1).

As we have shown in these two examples with the category of spirituality, the same attention to the severity of the symptoms that cause the behavioral impairment of the patient should be given to other categories, such as Lazarus' BASIC ID or Goldman et al.'s four spheres or levels (see Chapter 3). The following samples of patient impairment (Figures 10.3 and 10.4) correspond to each different model as they relate to Mr. D., whose case was described in detail in Chapter 2.

When it comes to writing a report for the managed care company that oversees the treatment of a particular patient, what the clinician has jotted down in the forms provided both in Chapter 3 and here will help in the composition of a clear statement that comprises the following 10 conditions, adapted once again from Goodman et al. (1992). The written report should (1) be as brief as

FIGURE 10.3

Impairment Severity

Following the Goodman, Brown, & Deitz (1992) model

Patient: Mr. D., 64 **Date:** 1/2/93

	Symptoms	Severity*
Biopsychology	Anxious (mostly) rumination	2
	Unable to concentrate	2
	Restless	2
Intimacy	Fears of wife's death (no cause)	1–2
People Interaction	(No problem)	0
Future Orientation	Worrying without reason about	
	finances	2–3
	Aging	
	Wife's dying	
Spirituality	OK, wants to help others and has	
	clear goals:	
	1. Books to read	
	2. European trip	
	3. Play clarinet	
	4. Offer consulting services	
	5. Teach sailing to youngsters	

Notes: Onset: Two months after sailing vacation with wife to celebrate retirement.

***Severity Level**

0 Absent
1 Moderate
2 Debilitating
3 Incapacitating
4 Dangerous!

FIGURE 10.4

Impairment Severity

Following the Lazarus (1981) model

Patient: Mr. D., 64 **Date:** 1/2/93

	Symptoms	Severity*
Behavior	Restless	2
	Unable to concentrate	2
Affect	Depressive, worrying	2–3
Sensations	Anxious, nervous	2
Images	Wife's death (She's in good health.)	1–2
	His old age incapacity (no cause)	2–3
Cognition	Worries about finances	2
Interpersonal	(No problem)	0
Diet	(No problem)	0
Spirituality	OK, desire to serve and has future goals:	0
	1. Books to read	
	2. European trip	
	3. Play clarinet	
	4. Offer consulting services	
	5. Teach sailing to youngsters	

Notes: Onset: Two months after sailing vacation with wife to celebrate retirement.

***Severity Level**

0 Absent
1 Moderate
2 Debilitating
3 Incapacitating
4 Dangerous!

possible, (2) be factual and descriptive, not interpretative or judgmental, (3) be nontheoretically biased, that is, written in neutral language, without terminology betraying adherence to a specific theoretical interpretation of symptoms or treatment techniques, (4) clearly explain the need for treatment, (5) describe the impairment within the larger picture of the patient's life, (6) adhere to DSM-IV diagnostic categories, (7) present, at least tentatively, a treatment plan, (8) consider the most effective, solution-oriented brief therapy treatment possible, (9) give clear rationale for the choice of that treatment plan, and (10) show openness for possible future modifications in treatment.

The more care is given to these categories, the better chances the clinician has to work cooperatively with managed care. And, obviously, the result of cooperative work with these companies will be less waste of time and energy for the practitioner and better service for the patient.

In order to exemplify the written reports for the managed care companies, we reproduce in its entirety the initial report on Mr. D. written after the first session. This is based on the Patient Impairment Severity forms for Mr. D., presented above. In the case of Mr. D., we used the Lazarus model form. These rough notes serve as a draft for the "official" written report.

Initial Report **Patient:** Mr. D. **Date:** 1/2/93

Mr. D.: 64, just retired after 20 years as President and CEO of own manufacturing company with which he had been for 34 years. Good health. Good marriage of 36 years, living with wife. Grown children, five grandchildren in NY area, where he lives from May to Sept. In FL from Oct. to Apr.

Onset: Two weeks after returning from sailing vacation in Caribbean. Started psychotherapy two months after onset.

Symptoms: Anxious most of the time. Restless and unable to concentrate on anything (even reading the paper). Preoccupied with nothing in particular and with things not related to him or his family. This makes him insecure and fearful. Sleep: wakes up worrying about his finances, though he knows his are in good order. In his words, "I worry about worrying. It never ends."

Impairment: Gets nothing done. Wastes time switching from task to task, not doing anything well, having no daily routine, and not doing the things that he wants to do.

Severity: Level 3 (Incapacitating).

Need for treatment: Psychotherapy is needed in order to avoid further deterioration that may end in clinical depression. His intact personality needs psychological support to adapt positively to the drastic change in his life caused by the retirement from a business that was an integral part of him for so many years.

Diagnosis: Adjustment Disorder with anxiety (DSM-IV: 309.24). There are clear indications that the psychosocial stressor that triggered this maladaptive reaction to his decision to retire was the drastic change in his lifestyle, from active President and CEO to retiree. This is a vicious cycle that psychotherapy can effectively and quickly break.

First Session: Patient related positively to therapist's corporate experience, but talked down to him, showing his disrespect for "management consultants" who have no direct experience with managing corporations. He demanded rapid results, no nonsense. Stressed that he was giving the therapist three sessions and no more to change him. Therapist agreed that in even one session patient should be able to experience some improvement and he put the responsibility of recovery in the patient's lap, explaining that he would be able to put into practice many of the things that he was going to *learn* with the therapist. The emphasis was on learning, not on medical cure.

When the therapist asked, "What comes to mind when you think of your current problem?" Mr. D. showed interest and said that he had never considered that. Then, quietly and pensively, admitted thoughts of growing old, useless and boring; feeling alone and afraid that his wife might die before him.
Patient was asked to focus his attention on concrete goals for the next five years. He had a ready list:

- Several books to read
- A long European trip to plan and take
- Learn to play the clarinet (a lifelong dream)
- Offer free business consultation to young businesspeople, through his church
- Teach sailing for free to poor youngsters in Florida

(Note: Mere coincidence of five goals for next five years).
Patient was encouraged to elaborate on these goals.

Prescription: To minimize the therapist role and strengthen the consultant function, the therapist recommended the reading of *Reengineering Yourself*, a self-help book for executives, with the comment that they would discuss it at the next appointment. Mr. D. was also asked to think of concrete ways to bring the five retirement goals closer to reality and to switch his thinking from any worrisome thoughts to thoughts of his goals, with as many concrete details and target dates as possible. These prescriptions were summarized in the following formula: Read, Plan, Switch.

Mr. D. left visibly satisfied and apologizing for his "rudeness" at the beginning of the first session.

This report, less than three typewritten pages long, gives a fairly accurate and direct description of Mr. D's. initial impairment, of his behavior during the first session, of the need for treatment, and even of some of his strengths. The report fulfills the 10 conditions mentioned above. It is (1) brief, (2) objective, (3) avoiding theoretical bias. (4) It gives reasons to validate psychotherapy as a special treatment modality, (5) describes the patient's impairment within the larger picture of his current existence, (6) uses DSM diagnostic categories, (7) gives some indication of a treatment plan (emphasizing learning rather than cure), (8) proposes Solution-Oriented Brief Therapy (SOBT) methods as shown by the prescriptions given to the very first session, (9) gives the rationale for (7 & 8) and, finally, (10) at least negatively, keeps the possibility of changes in the future depending on the patient's reactions to the initial prescriptions.

Another advantage of a well organized written report is that the clinician can always go back to it when asked by managed care to clarify any points of the report.

Because we have taken the idea of patient impairment severity levels from the work of Goodman et al. (1992), we again refer the clinician to their extraordinarily useful book.

The final item that the managed care companies need in order to know what they are paying for is related to the goals of treatment. This is accurately called *outcome objectives.* In other words, the treatment plan is directed to these goals, which will become the outcome of the treatment. In the case Mr. D., the goals that he proposed to himself for the retirement years helped the clinician establish the outcome objectives in the form of prescriptions. Thus, the prescriptions given him at the end of the session regarding bringing his five goals into the realm of execution became the objectives to start aiming at. These goals, summarized in the brief *Read, Plan, Switch* formula, become measurable and can be reported concretely and objectively, as was seen in Chapter 2.

Here, we merely want to emphasize that once goals have been established, the patient can then be encouraged to move towards them progressively. The information that the clinician should keep in order to be able to inform the managed care company in the next report refers to the same five goals. For instance, for Mr. D. the notes for the second therapy session indicate the following about the outcome objective.

> Patient started reading book assigned (three chapters) and began to practice what he read regarding constructive thinking. Has practiced five times in seven days the mind exercises found in these first three chapters of the book.
>
> Pt. contacted travel agent whom he knows and explained his desire to visit Europe for three months next year. Received packet of information in mail, but was unable to devote time to study them carefully.
>
> Contacted minister in his church and visited him regarding his two projects (Teach sailing; Offer free business consultation). Was disappointed with lukewarm and bureaucratic reception by minister. Will contact another, younger cleric.

The fact that the patient started to work on three of his five goals belongs to the outcome objectives. This is the result of his first session. Progress is being made regarding the impairments that brought him into therapy.

It is obvious that the goals (what to aim at) have a hierarchy determined by the severity of the symptoms that produce the patient impairment. Those of levels 4 and 3 must always be addressed first. The outcome objective (how well the patient has done in working towards the treatment goals) measures and reports the progress made. It should be noted, however, that in AD diagnoses the severity of the impairment very rarely reaches above the level between 2 and 3. When the severity is a definite 3 or 4, either behaviorally incapacitating the patient or creating imminent danger for self or others, the AD diagnosis has to be questioned and, most probably, modified.

11

Conclusion

This book, as well as this professional series, was prompted by the new clinical style of conducting psychotherapy imposed by the existence of managed care organizations (MCOs). This new reality has emerged as the enemy for many mental health services providers, to the point that is has become fashionable to blast MCOs when chitchatting with colleagues. Headlines in publications for professionals that sound ominous, such as "Economic terrorism prevents...resisting MCOs" (Bradman, 1994), and comments likening MCOs to dictatorships destroying the field of psychotherapy do not contribute to an objective view of what's happening.

Indeed, the MCO system is far from perfect and it needs much adjustment and reform. But no matter how much many clinicians regret that the good old times are gone, when the whole business of therapy (yes, business!) was between patient and provider, the big question now is whether to influence the system positively by trying to make it less imperfect or to reject it outright with the hope of destroying it.

On the side *against* MCOs is a dynamic interdisciplinary group, the "Coalition of Mental Health Professionals and Consumers," coordinated by Karen Shore, Ph.D., a competent, outspoken, and dedicated New York psychologist (see Saeman, 1994). On the side *in favor* of keeping MCOs basically as they are now, but changing the type and form used currently, we also find many responsible professionals.

Both positions should be understood dispassionately in order to make the right professional decisions and perhaps take full professional advantage of the present situation. What we have in mind is at both the clinical and the business levels of operation. This refers to providing the best possible quality care to patients, while being rewarded monetarily in as profitable a manner as is just and equitable for a professional mental health practitioner.

The con arguments are strong and well presented in order "to regulate managed care and to seek different solutions to replace managed care," in Dr. Shore's words, as quoted by Saeman (1994, p. 8). Two clusters of arguments against MCOs are usually presented: theoretical and managerial. The theory behind the opposition to the MCO's ways is ultimately rooted in psychoanalytical beliefs regarding psychotherapy and the interpersonal relationship between the clinician and the patient. Because of these beliefs, a completely different method like SOBT, mentioned several times throughout the book, is often considered shallow and ineffective, a dangerous shortcut in therapy, even though for more than two decades psychoanalysts like Sifneos (1979) and Strupp (1981), among others, have advocated short-term psychodynamic therapy. This is not the place to evaluate the merits of theoretical approaches, but we would simply argue against the cognitive and affective difficulties, coming from one's training, that some therapists find in accepting, or even tolerating, other modalities of dealing with mental health problems.

The managerial arguments against the MCO are many, most centered on the control that is now in the hands of these business organizations. Often, MCOs set arbitrary norms of their own in deciding what providers to admit into their network and how much each practitioner will be paid per session; they assign patients to clinicians without any consultation with the latter; they determine how many sessions are "necessary" in each case; they require periodic reports in their own complicated forms, with the information that they deem important; they require and expect the trust of the practitioner regarding confidentiality, since the MCOs do not report back to the clinician on how many people, trained in mental health practice or otherwise, will see, read, and even copy the reports submitted. The list goes on, including so-called blacklisting of practitioners who do not submit to their rules and regulations, wasted time in unnecessary paperwork, etc. All this is summarized by Shore, as quoted by Saeman (1994, p. 9): "It's immoral, it's iatrogenic, it hurts people, it's wrong."

The other camp, accepting the inevitability of MCOs and proposing changes in order to make the system work better for the benefit of both patients and practitioners, reviews the abuses in the heydays predating MCO, such as raising fees of service even when the expenses of providing services remained the same, or the practice of continuing therapy without clear goals in mind, or keeping poor and sloppy records and other such ways. Hebster (1994) claims that psychologists (and we add other mental health providers) can learn "the benefits and potential of an evolving healthcare system" (p. 14). Wylie (1994) also encourages therapists to "begin thinking big, putting more of their creative energies into issues that transcend their individual interests" (p. 33). Again, we can view their position from a theoretical as well as from a managerial point of view.

The theory used to justify the MCO concept is based on voluminous research data, as Hebster (1994) reminds us, that "continue to support that certain more time-intensive psychotherapeutic treatment approaches demonstrate similar outcomes when compared to brief, cost effective forms of treatment" (p. 14).

From the managerial point of view, the same author justifies MCOs in terms of the free market system and competition, without which, she claims, the old "system was doomed to fail" (p. 14). And she explains in the same place that "with the advent of prepaid insurance, a disincentive was created which neglected the need for the consumer to evaluate service on the basis of cost. Without this...inflation ensued in health care (which) has been far greater than in the economy as a whole." She continues to remind us that the noncompetitive market created an imbalance that sooner or later had to be corrected, and compares the current situation created by MCOs to the self-correction of the stock market that many people take for granted every day.

We are forced to conclude that the predictions against MCOs seem to be at best premature and at least a reflection of confusing the system as such with the way it is working at present. For instance, Bradman (1994) believes that "there is no doubt that, eventually, employers and other payers will see the wisdom of omitting this massive 'middle man' (managed care) and thereby maximizing cost effectiveness and value" (p. 10). In spite of this assertion, what will undoubtedly happen is a refinement of the system, a correction of its faults and imperfections. But the practical concept of overseeing how therapy is conducted is, in itself, sound and valid.

This book and the entire Brunner/Mazel Mental Health Practice Under Managed Care Series show what practitioners can do in constructive ways in order to work with MCOs and to benefit from doing so. The present confusion and discontent blamed on MCOs is part of the process of market adjustment mentioned above. Clinicians can use the energy spent in rebelling against the inevitable (the market corrects itself or collapses) in learning to work with MCOs. Instead of acting against the system as a whole, clinicians will benefit their work and will be able to "empower themselves by taking a leadership role in reforming the present...system," as Dr. Hebster reminds us in the same article.

As authors of the volume on Adjustment Disorders for this Managed Care series, we are bemused with the realization that managed care has become a matter of adjustment for many clinicians; in many cases, it has become a real disorder. In Chapters 6, 7, and 8, we discussed effective methods of treating this disorder. Should some of these be applied to themselves by those who find the MCO stressor overwhelming? Is this another case of "physician cure thyself"? Obviously, to insist on overthrowing the entire system, instead of working cooperatively to improve it for the benefit of everybody concerned, looks like that part of the AD symptomology that refers to the overreaction to the stressor. And because it is an overreaction, it becomes maladaptive and counterproductive.

Our personal position is very clear. Mental health professionals (and all health professionals for that matter) should not be exempt from checks and balances and from fair demands for productivity and general accountability. Something had to happen in view of the many excesses and abuses in the way mental health services were provided, charged to third party payers, and administered.

Managed care was born not merely out of the drive for profits by the insurance companies (though that gene was certainly part of their makeup), but also out of the arrogance of many mental health care providers. This arrogance included a "theoretical" refusal of accountability under the guise of patient confidentiality, the professions' inability to police themselves, the lack of rational norms at the entry level of professionalism, and other factors that belong at the very core of professional identity and respectability. These became bright red flashing lights for the insurance companies that were paying for the services rendered by these professionals whose house was (and still is) not in order.

We hope that this book will be a practical learning tool to *adjust* successfully to the new reality for which most practitioners were not trained, so that no AD diagnosis will be needed for mental healthcare providers.

Having said this, having "adjusted" to the current reality of mental health service delivery within the new requirements of managed care, we still want to stress the very important and crucial point made at the end of Chapter 8. In spite of the style of doing therapy imposed on clinicians nowadays, they cannot forget their humble role. Rather than to believe that they can "cure" patients, they might do better accepting the fact that total cure is a myth, that we are all "recovering," ever in the process of healing, adjusting, feeling existence, not just through our experiences of success, joy, and positivism, but also–and at times even more so–through those of war, disappointment, anxiety, and imagination's struggles, to use John Keats' items in his *Endymion.*

And clinicians will do well to remember what the same poem emphasizes, that these "negative" things are "All human; bearing in themselves this good,/ That they are still the air, the subtle food,/ To make us feel existence." Clinicians who believe that their role is "to cure," to do away with all struggle for their patients, to resolve all their problems, are denying the complexity of human existence and looking at it materially, mechanistically, as if humans can be fixed like machines.

Unfortunately, this is the most serious danger of the current managed care *attitude:* to believe that psychological problems can be fixed like a motor that can be tuned up or a diseased organ, like an appendix, that can be removed. Any form of *psycho*therapy is a learning process, a widening of one's view of human existence, accepting its frustrations, limitations, and hazards without believing that they will go away completely. And, paradoxically, this change in perception and expectations is what truly empowers humans to live fully.

The new way of doing therapy à la managed care, has, of course, not changed the reality of our human condition. Thus, the wise clinician will immunize himself/herself against the belief in anybody's ability to "cure" a patient in a few sessions. When we do psychotherapy, we are coaches, trainers, teachers, more than surgeons or physicians. We don't solve patients' problems; we help them find their own solutions. We don't cure; we help them activate their own inner resources of health and healing. We cannot truly help anybody unless we respect their own individuality–which means that people have different needs, recover at different speeds, and often cannot be squeezed into the statistical restrictions of the new way of managing mental health services.

Let the clinician keep the wisdom needed to enjoy and understand the complexities of being human, while adjusting constantly to the current modality of offering psychological services to patients.

References

Albert, G. (1991). *No fault living.* San Luis Obispo: Impact.

Allen, S. N. (1994). Psychological assessment of posttraumatic stress disorder: Psychosomatics, current trends and future directions. *The Psychiatric Clinics of North America, 8*, 327–350.

American Psychiatric Association. (1980). *Diagnostic and statistical manual of mental disorders* (3rd. ed.). Washington, DC: Author.

American Psychiatric Association. (1987). *Diagnostic and statistical manual of mental disorders* (3rd. ed., revised). Washington, DC: Author.

American Psychiatric Association. (1994). *Diagnostic and statistical manual of mental disorders* (4th. ed.). Washington, DC: Author.

Araoz, D. L. (1985). *The new hypnosis.* New York: Brunner/Mazel.

Araoz, D. L., & Sutton, W. S. (1994). *Reengineerinq yourself: A blueprint for personal success in the new corporate culture.* Holbrook, MA: Bob Adams.

Beck, A. T., Ward, C. H., Mendelson, M., Mock, J., & Erbough, J. (1961). An inventory for measuring depression. *Archives of General Psychiatry, 4*, 561–571.

Beck, A. T., Weisman, A., Lester, D., & Trexler, L. (1974). The measurement of pessimism: The hopelessness scale. *Journal of Consulting and Clinical Psychology, 42*, 861–865.

Beck, A. T., Epstein, N., Brown, G., & Steer, G. A. (1988). An inventory for measuring clinical anxiety: Psychosomatic properties. *Journal of Consulting and Clinical Psychology, 56*, 893–897.

Beck, A. T., & Freeman, A. (1990). *Cognitive therapy of personality disorders.* Boston: Allyn & Bacon.

Betz, N. E. (1987). Research training in counseling psychology: Have we addressed the real issues? *Counseling Psychologist, 14*, 107–113.

Bleck, R. T. (1993). *Give back the pain.* Bedford, MA: Mills & Sanderson.

Bradman, L. (1994). Fear of blacklisting, 'economic terrorism,' prevents many professionals from resisting MCOs. *The National Psychologist, 3*(4), 10–11.

Burte, J. M., & Acer, K. M. (1994). *The Burte-Acer Trauma Scale.* In preparation.

Caballo, V. E. (1988). *Teoria, evaluacion y entrenamiento de las habilidades sociales.* Valencia: Promolibro.

Caballo, V. E. (1991). *Manual de tecnicas y de terapia y modificacion de conducta.* Madrid: Siglo XXI.

Carnegie, D. (1944). *How to stop worrying and start living.* New York: Pocket Books.

Derogatis, L. R. (1983a). *SCL-90-R Version: Manual.* Baltimore, MD: John Hopkins Hospital.

Derogatis, L. R. (1983b). *SCL-90-R: Administration, scoring and procedure manual.* Towson, MD: Clinical Psychometric Research.

de Shazer, S. (1988). *Clues: Investigating solutions in brief therapy.* New York: W.W. Norton.

Dryden, W., & Ellis, A. (1986). Rational emotive therapy. In W. Dryden & W. Golden (Eds.), *Cognitive-behavioral approaches to psychotherapy.* London: Harper & Row.

Edelstien, M. G. (1990). *Symptom analysis: A method of brief therapy.* New York: W.W. Norton.

Ellis, A. (1962). *Reason and emotion in psychotherapy.* Secaucus, NJ: Citadel.

Ellis, A. (1986). Rational-emotive behavior therapy applied to relationship therapy. *Journal of Rational-Emotive Therapy*, 4–21.

Epstein, S., & Brodsky, A. (1993). *You're smarter than you think: How to develop your practical intelligence for success in living.* New York: Simon & Schuster.

Epstein, S. (1994). Integration of the cognitive and the psychodynamic unconscious. *American Psychologist, 49*, 709–724.

Fabrega, H., Jr., Mezziah, J. E., & Mezziah, A. C. C. (1987). Adjustment disorder as a marginal or transitional illness category in DSM-III. *Archives of General Psychiatry, 44*, 657–672.

Fox, R. (1987). Short-term, goal-oriented therapy. *Social Casework: The Journal of Contemporary Social Work, 68*, 494–499.

Gilligan, S. G. (1990). Coevolution of primary process in brief therapy. In J. K. Zeig & S. G. Gilligan (Eds.), *Brief therapy: Myths, methods and metaphors.* New York: Brunner/Mazel.

Goodman, M., Brown, J., & Deitz, P. (1992). *Managing managed care: A mental health practitioner's survival guide.* Washington, DC: American Psychiatric Association.

Gordon, D. (1990). Reference experiences: Guardians of coherence and instigators of change. In J. K. Zeig & S. G. Gilligan (Eds.), *Brief therapy: Myths, methods and metaphors.* New York: Brunner/Mazel.

Gustafson, J. P. (1990). The great simplifying conventions of brief individual psychotherapy. In J. K. Zeig & S. G. Gilligan (Eds.), *Brief therapy: Myths, methods and metaphors.* New York: Brunner/Mazel.

Haley, J. (1990). Why not long-term therapy? In J. K. Zeig & S. G. Gilligan (Eds.), *Brief therapy: Myths, methods and metaphors.* New York: Brunner/Mazel.

Hall, D. P., Jr., & Benedek, D. M. (1993). Adjustment disorder criteria. *Hospital and Community Psychiatry, 44*, 592–595.

Hathaway, S. R., & McKinley, J. C. (1989). *Manual for administration and scoring MMPI-2.* Minneapolis, MN: Minnesota Press.

Hays, R. B., & Oxley, D. (1986). Social network development and functioning during a life transition. *Journal of Personality and Social Psychology, 50*, 305–313.

Hebster, C. (1994). Despite managed care, opportunities abound as never before. *The National Psychologist, 3*(6), 14.

Joint Commission on Accreditation of Healthcare Organizations (1991). *Consolidated Standards Manual* (Vol. 1: Standards). Oakbrook Terrace, IL: Author.

Korn, E. R., & Pratt, G. J. (1987). *Hyper-performance: The A.I.M. strategy for releasing your business potential.* New York: John Wiley & Sons.

Kushel, G. (1994). *Reaching the peak performance zone.* New York: American Management Association, AMACOM.

Lazarus, A. (1981). *The practice of multi-modal therapy.* New York: McGraw-Hill.

Madanes, C. (1990). Strategies and metaphors in brief therapy. In J. K. Zeig & S. G. Gilligan (Eds.), *Brief therapy: Myths, methods and metaphors.* New York: Brunner/Mazel.

Mahoney, M. J. (1992). *Human change processes.* New York: Basic Books.

Meichenbaum, D. (1977). *Cognitive behavior modification.* New York: Plenum.

Meichenbaum, D. (1994). *A clinical handbook/practical therapist manual for assessing and treating adults with posttraumatic stress disorder.* Toronto: Institute Press.

Moore, T. (1994). *Care of the soul.* New York: HarperCollins.

Napier, N. J. (1990). *Recreating your self.* New York: W. W. Norton.

Oldham, J. M., & Morris, L. B. (1990). *Personality self-portrait.* New York: Bantam Books.

Peale, N. V. (1974). *You can if you think you can.* New York: Fawcett Crest.

Polster, E. (1990). Tight therapeutic sequences. In J. K. Zeig & S. G. Gilligan

(Eds.), *Brief therapy: Myths, methods and metaphors.* New York: Brunner/Mazel.

Resnick, H. S. (1988). Malingering and posttraumatic disorders. In R. Rogers (Ed.), *Clinical assessment of malingering and deception.* New York: Guilford Press.

Rogers, R. (Ed.). (1988). *Clinical assessment of malingering and deception.* New York: Guilford Press.

Saeman, H. (1994). Managed care likened to dictatorships which purge foes. *The National Psychologist, 3*(6), 8–9.

Schwartz, D. J. (1959). *The magic of thinking big.* New York: Cornerstone Library.

Shatzberg, A. F. (1990). Anxiety and adjustment disorder: A treatment approach. *Journal of Clinical Psychiatry, 51*(11), supplement, 20–24.

Sherman, R., Oresky, P., & Rountree, Y. (1991). *Solving problems in couple and family therapy: Techniques and tactics.* New York: Brunner/Mazel.

Sifneos, P. (1979). *Short-term dynamic psychotherapy: Evaluation and technique.* New York: Plenum.

Smith, D. (1982). Trends in counseling and psychotherapy. *American Psychologist, 37,* 352–358.

Spielberger, C. D., Gorsuch, R. L., & Lushene, R. F. (1970). *Manual for state trait anxiety inventory.* Palo Alto, CA: Consulting Psychologists Press.

Stone, W. C. (1962). *The success system that never fails.* New York: Pocket Books.

Strain, J. J., Newcorn, J., Wolf, D., & Fulop, G. (1993). Considering changes in adjustment disorder. *Hospital and Community Psychiatry, 44,* 13–15.

Strupp, H. H. (1981). Toward a refinement of time-limited dynamic psychotherapy. In S. Budman (Ed.), *Forms of brief therapy.* New York: Guilford Press.

Watzlawick, P., Weakland, J., & Fisch, R. (1974). *Change: Principles of problem formation and problem resolution.* New York: W. W. Norton.

Weed, L. L. (1969). *Medical records medical education and patient care.* Cleveland: Case Western Reserve University Press.

World Health Organization. (1978). *International Classification of Diseases* (9th. revision). Geneva: World Health Organization.

Wylie, M. S. (1994). Endangered species. *Family Networker,* March/April, 21–23.

Zeig, J. K. (1994). Advanced techniques of utilization. In J. K. Zeig (Ed.), *Ericksonian methods: The essence of the story.* New York: Brunner/Mazel.

Zeig, J. K., & Gilligan, S. G. (Eds.). (1990). *Brief therapy: Myths, methods and metaphors.* New York: Brunner/Mazel.

Name Index

Albert, G., 104
Araoz, D. L., 33, 104, 106

Beck, A. T., 66
Bleck, R. T., 104
Bradman, L., 148, 151
Brodsky, A., 139
Brown, J., ix, 24, 30, 137, 142

Caballo, V. E., 66
Carnegie, D., 104

Deitz, P., ix, 24, 30, 137, 142
de Shazer, S., 129, 130

Edelstien, M. G., 25
Ellis, A., 66, 71, 104
Epstein, S., 85, 112, 118, 139
Erickson, M. H., 76

Fisch, R., 74
Fox, R., 128, 129
Freeman, A., 66

Gilligan, S. G., 67, 76
Goodman, M., ix, 22, 24, 25, 26, 27, 28, 29, 30, 31, 33, 127, 136, 137, 139, 140, 141, 142
Gordon, D., 67
Gustafson, J. P., 67

Haley, J., 67
Hebster, C., 150, 151

Keats, J., 122, 152
Korn, E. R., 104
Kushel, G., 104

Lazarus, A., ix, 25, 26, 28, 29, 30, 31, 138, 139, 141, 144

Mahoney, M. J., 66
Meichenbaum, D., 66
Moore, T., 122
Morris, L. B., 50, 52-54

Napier, N. J., 116

Oldham, J. M., 50, 52–54
Oresky, P., 126

Peale, N. V., 104
Polster, E., 67
Pratt, G. J., 104

Ramon the Campoamor, 6
Rogers, C., 4
Roundtree, Y., 126

Saeman, H., 148, 150
Schwartz, D. J., 104
Sherman, R., 126
Shore, K., 148, 149
Sifneos, P., 149
Stone, W. C., 104
Strupp, H. H., 149
Sutton, W. S., 33, 104

Watzlawick, P., 74
Weakland, J., 74
Weed, L. L., 135, 136
Wylie, M. S., 4, 150

Zeig, J. K., 76

Subject Index

Acute/chronic distinction, case illustration, 20
Adjustment Disorders
case illustration, 11–23
cultural variables and, 5–9
diagnosis of, 34–48. *See also* Diagnosis
DSM–IV and, 1–2, 3, 5, 8–9
managed care and, 4–5
self-therapy for, 104–123
spirituality and, 141–147
treatment principles, 65–76
Anxiety, Adjustment Disorder with, 36–37, 40

Bereavement, 75
Bibliotherapy
case illustration, 16, 20
self-therapy, 104. *See also* Self-therapy
Biopsychology, patient impairment, 26, 27
Brief Therapy model, treatment principles, 67, 68
BRIMS, treatment, 99–103
Color breathing, self-therapy, 116–118
Communications, with managed care companies, 31–33
Conduct Disturbance, Adjustment Disorder with, 37, 41
Consolidated Standards Manual (JCAHO), 128
Constructive action, treatment principles, 70–71
Cultural variables
Adjustment Disorders and, 5–9
diagnosis and, 35

Depressed Mood, Adjustment Disorder with, 36, 40
Depressed Mood and Mixed Anxiety, Adjustment Disorder with, 37, 41
Diagnosis, 34–48
case illustrations, 42–48
checklist for, 39–41
overview of, 34–35
Personality Disorders, 49–64
case illustrations, 54–64
overview of, 49–54
tentative, 35–38
Dream analysis, case illustration, 13, 14
DSM-IV
acute/chronic distinction, 20
Adjustment Disorders and, 1–2, 3, 5, 8–9

cultural variables and, 6, 7
diagnosis and, 34
patient impairment, 24, 27
Personality Disorders, diagnosis
case illustrations, 54–64
overview of, 49–54
tentative diagnosis, 35–38

Functional impairment, emphasis on, 2
Future orientation, patient impairment, 26, 28

Hidden symptom, self-therapy, 105–107

Impairment. *See* Patient impairment
International Classification of Diseases (WHO), 1
Interpersonal relationships, patient impairment, 28
Intimate relationships, patient impairment, 28

Longer-term psychotherapy, described, 124–134

Malingering, 90
Managed care, 1–10
Adjustment Disorders and, 4–5
adjustment to, 148–153
communications and, 31–33
constraints of, 2–4
cultural variables and, 5–9
DSM-IV and, 1–2
longer-term psychotherapy, 124, 127–134
spirituality and, in communication with, 135–147
Medical model
Adjustment Disorders and, 4–5
managed care and, 4
Mental rehearsal, self-therapy, 109–110
Mental self defense, self-therapy, 115–116
Mixed Anxiety and Depressed Mood, Adjustment Disorder with, 36–37, 41
Multimodal Behavior Therapy
model of, 26–31
patient impairment, 25

Patient impairment, 24–33
models of, 26–31
overview of, 24–26
Patient Impairment Profile (P.I.P.), 26, 29–31
People interaction, patient impairment, 26
Perception, treatment principles, 69
Personality
hidden symptom, self-therapy, 106–107
resistance and, 126
Personality Disorders
diagnosis, 49–64
case illustrations, 54–64
overview of, 49–54
symptoms, 35
Pharmacology, case illustration, 15
Posttraumatic and/or Acute Stress Disorder, symptoms, 35, 75
Prescriptions, self-therapy, 119–123
Psychotherapy, 77–103
detailed outline of, 82–103
longer-term, 124–134
self-therapy, 104–123
summary outline of, 77–82
treatment principles, 65–76

Rational Emotive Therapy
Adjustment Disorders, 85
self-therapy and, 113
treatment principles, 66, 70
Reframing, treatment principles, 69–70, 95
Resistance, Solution-Oriented Brief Therapy (SOBT), 125–126
Responsibility, treatment principles, 70–71
Role model, self-therapy, 113–115

Self-therapy, 104–123. *See also* Bibliotherapy
- color breathing, 116–118
- future emphasis, 108
- hidden symptom, 105–107
- mental rehearsal, 109–110
- mental self defense, 115–116
- overview of, 104–105
- past accomplishments, 112–113
- prescriptions, 119–123
- role model, 113–115
- somatic bridge, 111–112
- weekly schedule form, 120

Solution-Oriented Brief Therapy (SOBT)
- acute/chronic distinction, 20
- adaptations of, 103
- case illustration, 16
- longer-term therapy, 125–126

Somatic bridge, self-therapy, 111–112

Spirituality, in communication with managed care, 135–147

Suicide, cultural variables and, 6, 7

Tentative diagnosis, 35–38. *See also* Diagnosis

Thoughts, treatment principles, 70

Treatment principles, 65–76. *See also* Psychotherapy

World Health Organization, 1